DREAMLAND

How Canada's Pretend Foreign Policy Has Undermined Sovereignty

– by Roy Rempel –

BREAKOUT
educational network

PUBLISHED FOR

BREAKOUT EDUCATIONAL NETWORK

AND THE

SCHOOL OF POLICY STUDIES, QUEEN'S UNIVERSITY

BY MCGILL-QUEEN'S UNIVERSITY PRESS

MONTREAL & KINGSTON – LONDON – ITHACA

Publisher: Inta D. Erwin
Copy-editor: Loretta Johnson, First Folio Resource Group, Inc.
Production Editor: Bob Templeton, First Folio Resource Group, Inc.
Layout and Design: Greg Duhaney, First Folio Resource Group, Inc.
Book Cover: Mark Howes

Library and Archives Canada Cataloguing in Publication

Rempel, Roy, 1962–
  Dreamland: how Canada's pretend foreign policy has undermined sovereignty/by Roy Rempel.

Includes bibliographical references and index.

ISBN 1-55339-119-5 (bound).–ISBN 1-55339-118-7 (pbk.)

1. Canada–Foreign relations–1945-. 2. Canada–Foreign
relations–United States. 3. United States–Foreign relations–Canada. I. Queen's University (Kingston, Ont.). School of Policy Studies II. Breakout Educational Network III. Title.

FC242.R45 2006   327.71'009'072
C2006-901196-6

Printed and bound in Canada.

Canadian broadcast rights for the *underground royal commission* report and the *urc* Investigates.

To subscribe to ichannel contact your local cable service provider.
Visit the *urc* Web site link at:
www.ichanneltv.com

TABLE OF CONTENTS

ACKNOWLEDGEMENTS

At some point in the future, Canada may face a major crisis only to find that its capability to respond is seriously wanting. If such an event occurs, it is likely that calls will be made for a public inquiry, or even for a Royal Commission, to look into how this could have happened.

But do we really need to wait for such a crisis? The gaps in Canada's various national capabilities, and in the way in which we make decisions, have already been exposed in numerous studies and reports. A particularly holistic analysis of the state of our national political institutions has already been undertaken by the underground royal commission (urc). In this regard, I am indebted to the work of Kitson Vincent and the urc for informing the analysis contained in this book. The vast body of work undertaken by the urc over the past several years, encompassing books and documentaries, exposes that policy-making in Canada is ubiquitously lacking in accountability; a weak connection between the electors and the elected means that we are slowly and irrevocably losing the right to know our government.

This is particularly evident in the realm of international policy where power is concentrated in the hands of only a few individuals. The urc documentary *Question of Honour* exposes that Canadian defence policy of recent years has often been detached from the everyday realities faced by Canadian troops in the field. At the same time, the national interest has, all too often, been completely absent from the process of policy-making. The roots of these policy shortcomings are not simply found in an absence of resources. Rather, they are cultural and institutional.

The contributions made by several members of the urc to this manuscript have been invaluable. Dr. Douglas Bland of Queen's University commented on early drafts of the manuscript and greatly assisted in shaping the analysis. The research and teaching work that we have been able to undertake together related to Canada's strategic culture has also been instrumental in contributing to the content of this book.

Dr. John Robson greatly assisted with the editing process, and further contributions were made by Alan Williams, Paul Kemp, Kaylie Wells, Robert Roy, Criss Hajek, and Inta Erwin. I am indebted to each of them for their valuable inputs and support.

As always, however, any errors or omissions that may be found in this book are entirely my own responsibility.

Roy Rempel

FOREWORD

Every country has two versions of its foreign policy. There is the version that other countries and non-state actors see; and the domestic version, that its citizens see. While neither version is necessarily more truthful than the other, there is a risk to any country when the gap between the two versions becomes too large. A puffed-up foreign policy abroad, without support or material engagement from home, is just as dangerous as a Potemkin-village foreign policy at home that has no salience or credibility abroad.

Canada has a history of working with varying levels of success to manage this gap. Some governments, hoping to operate on old myths, devoid of any real commitment to provide material support for the key elements of defence, development, or diplomacy, created in Canada, a sense of our respected standing abroad that was severely detached from reality. Other governments, wishing to avoid debate on our real foreign and defence capacities, have poked at the piñata of anti-American sentiment, always available in Canada since 1776. On the other side of the ledger, some governments have over-reached themselves in support of defence, multi-lateral, or development goals, and then, despite a sincere commitment, been unable to deliver fiscally.

In the past, Canada has shown a remarkable commitment to the defence of freedom. In peace and war, notably the two world wars, Canadian forces have performed acts of heroism and duty, and my generation is genuinely grateful to those who made great sacrifice for our way of life. Today, however, few Canadians have any first-hand experience of war. The absence of this experience is a tribute to the success of initiatives like NATO and NORAD. Canada has stood with other Atlantic allies to assert real military commitments on the ground, in the air, and on the seas, determined to destroy any enemy who sought to launch a nuclear or military attack against our allies or ourselves. Without a shot being fired, the standoff between two thermonuclear alliances was resolved in a way that liberated old Soviet satellites in Europe and Eurasia while facilitating the beginnings of democracy in Russia and elsewhere.

Our task then, as Canadians, was to stand fast and struggle to do our share. There were setbacks; but, by and large, we discharged our duties in the same way as we led the peacekeeping role in the post-Korean War, UN-sphere of influence in places like the Congo, Cyprus, the Middle East, and elsewhere.

But the end of the Cold War has also liberated other forces in various parts of the world that do not respond to the old rules and the traditional alliance postures. This result has necessitated a re-thinking of both doctrine and practice—and an enthusiastic debate and engagement on that front. The activities of the Standing Committee on National Defence in the House, the Foreign Relations Committee of the House, the Senate Committees on National Defence and Security and on Foreign Affairs, all contributed to that debate, in a remarkably nonpartisan and blunt fashion. Think tanks, university researchers, and scholars also weighed in with opinions from the right and the left, as well as those that were of a more purely empirical nature. Canada's allies, notably the United Kingdom and the United States, were also not silent on the choices we faced and the imperatives we needed to address.

The ideas and reflections in this book, many of which I agree with and some of which I do not, are all important parts of the continuing debate in Canada about closing the gap between the two versions of our foreign policy. At the time of writing, we have a new chief of the Defence Staff who seems very much aware of the tougher, more multi-polar, and asymmetrical threat faced by our national security; and a newly elected minority Conservative government, with a long record of advocating a more robust commitment to the increased complement, training, kit, and new fighting and lift platforms that a viable and deployable modern force must have. Still, choosing a direction and implementing it effectively are two very separate tasks.

Also at the time of writing, the bureaucratic battle over procurement has just begun in earnest. Competing lobbyists, just doing their jobs, and who all have the unique right answer, are also fully engaged, as befits a competitive political and economic environment. This book is a timely reminder to politicians, academics, bureaucrats, lobbyists, and senior officers that the gaps between intended and real capacity are genuine, the need for resolution is intense, and the misleading and illusory elements of our foreign policy over the last decade or so have had a real cost, which is only aggravated by undue delay.

I am profoundly more optimistic and positive than aspects of what you are about to read; but that optimism does not diminish my own conviction that the debate that the ideas and analysis in this book will generate is profoundly healthy for the body politic and Canada's right choices ahead to best protect and advance our geopolitical interests—be they security, humanitarian, economic, or social—and the ways those interests effectively reflect the values we share as Canadians.

Hon. Hugh D. Segal, C.M.
The Senate of Canada
Ottawa

INTRODUCTION

From Partner to Protectorate

*defy you to find any minister... who invests time and effort in the
Canada/U.S. relationship to a degree that is at all commensurate
with its importance to the economy.*

–John Manley, former deputy prime minister

At the end of June 2002, Abitibi-Consolidated closed down 22 of its saw
mills in British Columbia and Quebec, putting 5,000 Canadians out of
work. The cause of the mill closings was the duty placed on Canadian
softwood imports by the United States. By 2005, the ongoing softwood
dispute had cost Canadian industry $5 billion in duties and billions
more in lost sales.[1] On the day after the mills closed in 2002, Canada
Day, the Department of Foreign Affairs and International Trade issued
only one statement—it welcomed the creation of the International
Criminal Court (ICC).[2]

Since 2001, the softwood issue has been a sore point in Canada-U.S.
relations. Although the United States reduced some of its duties late in
2005, immense damage has been done to the Canadian softwood industry and this will likely continue for some time.[3] While the government
tried to rely on the dispute settlement mechanisms of the North
American Free Trade Agreement (NAFTA) to resolve the dispute, its
broader foreign policy agenda sought to find issues that create greater
political distance between Canada and the United States—the ICC, Iraq
and missile defence were all issues over which the Canadian and U.S. governments clashed. The result was that the broader political relationship
between the two governments did not create the right environment for
resolving the dispute quickly.

Over the past decade, Canadian foreign policy has emphasized those
issues in which Canada is said to play a unique role in the world. Former
prime minister Martin's introduction to the 2005 International Policy

Statement (IPS) illustrates this when he says, in his very first sentence, that: "Foreign policy is how a nation best expresses itself to the world."[4] Many Canadians who pay attention are used to thinking in the same way. When many Canadians think about foreign policy, they think about diplomatic initiatives such as the one that created the ICC, about Canada's role in peacekeeping, or about Canadian aid to Africa.

While this approach to foreign policy may appear to be innocuous, it does Canada a great disservice. "Playing a role" or "expressing the national character" overseas is not the *raison d'etre* of foreign policy. Instead, the centre of gravity of any state's international policy should be wherever the livelihood and well-being of ordinary citizens are most affected by international events. An international policy that downplays that reality and instead seeks to "express Canada to the world" may sound good to some, but it is largely irrelevant to the needs of most Canadians.

A former Canadian ambassador to the United States, Derek Burney, has referred to this approach as Canada's "pretend foreign policy."[5] Driven by the desire for domestic political gain and the ideology of national leaders, Canada's international policy has become disconnected from the reality of the country's international position and from real national needs. What is discretionary, irrelevant, or even counter to the country's real interests has become central; what is most important to ordinary Canadians is too often ignored.

The most serious consequence of this policy approach is that it has marginalized Canada exactly where our influence most matters—the United States. This book argues that owing to this style of foreign policy Canada is in the process of becoming little more than a *de facto* protectorate, rather than independent partner, of the United States. This marked strategic and political decay of the country should be a subject of pressing concern for the new Harper government.

Ignoring Strategic Realities

My assessment might seem alarmist. Isn't Canada a member of the G8 group of leading industrialized countries[6], the seventh largest contributor to the UN budget (out of 191 member states), and the seventh highest military spender among NATO's 26 members?[7] Official government statements continually refer to Canada's pivotal importance internationally. For instance, the 1995 Foreign Policy White Paper claims:

Canada occupies a position of leadership among the open, advanced societies which are becoming increasingly influential as world power is dispersing and becoming more defined in economic terms. ... Canada can further its global interests better than any other country through its active membership in key international groupings.[8]

However, Canada's international position must always be considered in the context of its geo-strategic position; namely that it is a North American power situated next to the United States. Neither diplomatic activity at the UN nor the money spent on one international enterprise or another are indicative of real rank in the international system, particularly when such activity or spending does not translate into real capability or diplomatic weight where it most matters—in Washington, and with other states that are the key players in the international system.

While many Canadians have tended to ignore the realities of Canada's geo-strategic position in favour of activity in international organizations, recent studies of our international role have expressed very similar and common themes: that the country's international influence is declining; that the ability of Canada to "make a difference" internationally is not what it once was; even that Canada's national independence may be at stake.

To address this problem, the Martin government's International Policy Statement of 2005 was conceived as a blueprint for putting Canada back on track; in the words of the IPS, to enable the country to "make a difference" and to "fulfill its global potential."[9]

However, the dilemmas that confront Canada's international policy are really much more fundamental than a simple "loss of influence." Canada is becoming internationally irrelevant. Within North America, it is at risk of becoming little more than an "object" rather than an independent "actor" in terms of its relationship with the United States. That reality, in turn, will define the nature of Canada's broader international position and influence.

This problem is not easily remedied. Increased spending on defence, foreign aid, or diplomacy for instance, will not matter if the political commitment is temporary or if it is set on a weak policy foundation. All too often in the past, attempts to reinvigorate the country's international influence have foundered for exactly those reasons.

Canadian international policy faces a more fundamental problem that is cultural in nature. Canadians believe that what we do internationally is discretionary; that is, in the words of former prime minister Paul Martin, international policy is merely an expression of our national values and character. This approach means that all too often, and to our detriment, we have ignored our real national interests; in other words, what really matters.

If we are to regain such international effectiveness as our size, position, and circumstances permit, then a national culture and institutions that restore realism to policymaking must be the starting point.

Narrowing Our Policy Space by Ignoring the National Interest

Clearly defined national interest objectives are the only foundation for credible international policy. Specific international policy goals flow from interests that in turn define the national capabilities (military, diplomatic, aid, and intelligence) that are required. These capability requirements then serve as the basis for the allocation of national resources.

In this regard, an interesting contrast with Canada is Australia. When Australia released its 2003 Foreign Policy White Paper, the *raison d'etre* of its international policy was expressed without any ambiguity:

> The **purpose** of Australian foreign and trade policy is to advance the national interest—the security and prosperity of Australia and Australians. The **task** of Australia's foreign and trade policy is to advocate and advance those interests in a way which is both effective and in accord with the values of the Australian people [emphasis in the original].[10]

Such clarity that relates ends to means has been almost entirely absent from Canada's international policy of recent years. Indeed, the term "the national interest" is rarely used, let alone discussed, in Canada. Not only is it is absent from government documents, it rarely appears in most academic writing on the subject of international policy.

Instead of basing policy goals on the national interest, it is "values" that have come to serve as the foundation for Canadian foreign policy. But values such as democracy, human rights, and the rule of law (all central in government policy statements) are continuously engaged everywhere. They offer few bases on which to make choices. For a smaller power, such as Canada, this has led to an international policy in which everything is a priority, where resources are widely dispersed to support a multitude of goals, and in which there is large-scale ambivalence and lack of understanding about the nature of power and the sources of real influence in international affairs.

The promotion of common strategic and economic interests has an additional benefit; it is an important source of national unity. Both Quebecers and British Columbians either benefit or suffer equally as a result of the state of the softwood lumber trade between Canada and the United States. Interests serve as a bridge between divergent value systems, among different regions of the country and among provinces. Values and value systems often differ, but interests unite.

Canada's values-based policy has deliberately sought to establish political distance between Canada and the United States. Instead of crafting an international policy that uses the Canada-U.S. relationship for national advantage, Canadian leaders have tried to do exactly the opposite. Over the past decade in particular, anti-Americanism has come to characterize the attitudes of many Canadian leaders. This means that for many Americans, even though basic Canadian and American values and strategic interests remain closely analogous, the *reason* to maintain a real partnership with Canada is increasingly absent. For Canada, the consequence of declining American support has been stillborn diplomatic initiatives, declining political leverage where it matters most, and an erosion of national sovereignty.

Two Alternatives: Protectorate or Partnership

Some will consider it ironic, but the only way for Canada to sustain real independence in North America is to maintain an effective partnership with the United States. A partnership relationship affords Canada the ability to advance its own tactical interests and objectives in a bilateral context; a protectorate relationship does not. A partnership relationship between Canada and the United States is also Canada's most important vehicle for enhancing its influence internationally. As Derek Burney comments, "Canada can often have greater influence in global affairs when it is perceived as having a position of respect or privilege in Washington."[11] The closer that relationship is, the more seriously Canada will be taken by other states in the international system.

Any real partnership is grounded in good faith, mutual respect, understanding, and shared decision making. This is even more important when the relationship between two states is asymmetrical—that is, characterized by vast differences in power. A partnership between two states of widely divergent power cannot be maintained in circumstances in which the larger state begins to lose confidence in the smaller one. In those circumstances, the absence of good faith will cause the larger state to begin to move ahead unilaterally, and where necessary, to simply impose its will on the smaller state.

For nearly 60 years Canada was considered a partner by the United States, but that position has been progressively eroded. Ideologically motivated Canadian political initiatives, seen as harmful to American interests, and a chronic indifference to matters of national defence, have driven a wedge between the two countries.

This has been a grave mistake. From an interest-based perspective, it should never matter to Canadians who happens to occupy the White House at a given moment in time; nor should it matter which party happens to control Congress. The only thing that matters is the continuous requirement to ensure that the relationship between Canada and the United States is one in which the national interest, centred on the prosperity and well-being of Canadians, can be effectively advanced.

Canada's present approach to international policy is self-defeating. If Canada is to move away from becoming a protectorate and instead reestablish a true partnership with the U.S., that reality, and the reasons for it, must first be recognized and addressed.

****

Part I of this book outlines the problem: the archetypal ineptitude of recent Canadian policy on ballistic missile defence and key central myths of recent Canadian foreign policy, all demonstrably false, that underpin not merely the rhetoric but also the actions of policy-makers. The book also examines the consequences of the running down of Canada's international policy capabilities. Part II offers solutions, beginning with a recognition of the seriousness of the problem, followed by three case studies of how other middle powers have conducted more effective diplomacy, and then the institutional and intellectual reforms necessary to our doing the same. The ultimate objective is by no means an easy one, but it is essential: to begin to change our national strategic culture and think seriously about Canada's national interests and how to advance them for the collective benefit of all Canadians.

—NOTES—

[1] CBC News online: "Abitibi-Consolidated Closing Mills Due to Softwood Duties" (June 25, 2002); CTV.ca online: "NAFTA Panel Sides with Canada in Lumber Dispute" (August 10, 2005).

[2] Department of Foreign Affairs and International Trade. "Canada Welcomes Creation of International Criminal Court" (July 1, 2002)

[3] The U.S. Senate voted (by one vote) to repeal the so-called Byrd amendment in December 2005. However, the controversial law (by which Canadian duties are used to subsidize the U.S. softwood industry) is still expected to remain in force until at least October 2007. Fordaq "U.S. Senate votes to repeal Byrd amendment" (December 22, 2005)
[http://www.fordaq.com/fordaq/Senate_Byrd_Amendment_2390.html]

[4] Canada. *Canada's International Policy Statement: A Role of Pride and Influence in the World* Overview
Paper (2005) Forward from the Prime Minister

[5] Derek H. Burney, "Foreign Policy: More Coherence, Less Pretence" (Simon Riesman Lecture in International Trade Policy, Carleton University, March 14, 2005) p. 16.

[6] Along with the United States, Japan, Germany, France, the United Kingdom, Italy, and Russia.

[7] Source: Foreign Affairs Canada and Department of National Defence.

[8] Canada. Department of Foreign Affairs and International Trade, *Canada in the World*, (Ottawa: Public Works and Government Services Canada, 1995) p. i.

[9] Canada. *Canada's International Policy Statement: A Role of Pride and Influence in the World* Overview
Paper (2005) p. 5

[10] Australia, Department of Foreign Affairs and Trade, *Advancing the National Interest: Australia's Foreign and Trade Policy White Paper* (February 2003) p. vii.

[11] D.H. Burney "Canada-US Relations: Promise Pending?" *In the Canadian Interest? Assessing Canada's International Policy Statement* (Canadian Defence and Foreign Affairs Institute, November 2005) p. 12

CHAPTER 1

Ballistic Missile Defence and the Drift
Toward Protectorate Status

*We simply cannot understand why Canada would, in effect,
give up its sovereignty–its seat at the table.*

–Paul Cellucci, former U.S. Ambassador to Canada

On a cold day in November 2004, an interceptor missile was quietly installed in its underground silo at Fort Greely, Alaska. It completed "phase one" of an American ground-based ballistic missile defence (BMD) system. A few months later this system was declared operational.

The objective of BMD has been clear since the early Clinton years: to protect the United States against possible limited ballistic missile attack by rogue states. It has also been clear that whatever its merits, it enjoys strong bipartisan support in the United States at the presidential and the congressional level. And Canadian decision makers have long been aware of its importance. The 1994 Canadian Defence White Paper confirmed Canada's "interest" in "gaining a better understanding of missile defence through research and in consultation with like-minded nations."[1] Despite this significant advance warning, BMD was ultimately handled in an intellectually inept manner that alienated the Americans to no discernable purpose.

The basic cause of the missile defence debacle was the failure of the Chrétien government to approach the BMD issue from any sort of Canadian interest perspective. It did not ask whether BMD would help protect Canada directly, nor whether limited Canadian participation would help protect us indirectly by improving relations with Washington at little cost. Instead, the government's approach was based on a strange commitment to a 1972 treaty (the Anti-Ballistic Missile Defence agreement) to which Canada was not even a signatory and by a kind of visceral opposition to "things military." As then foreign minister Lloyd Axworthy told the *Washington Post* in 2000:

> We have expressed very strong concerns that any movement of the national missile defence that abrogates the ABM Treaty would be wrong. We don't like anything that would further expand acceleration of missile capacity.[2]

Decision-Making on the Fly

When the Martin government took office in December 2003, it initially seemed to signal a shift in attitude. Shortly before becoming prime minister, Paul Martin said: "I think our sovereignty depends on our being at the table when discussions are taking place about the defence of North America."[3] The new approach seemed better tailored to several strategic realities:

- All potential flight paths of missiles that might be fired by rogue states at the United States pass over Canadian territory.
- Active engagement in the evolution of BMD might allow Canada some ability to influence the parameters of its research in ways that protect Canadian political and security interests.
- Missiles can reach North America from almost any point on Earth in only about 30 minutes, so Canadian representation in the missile defence command structure is vital to our having any say in launch decisions.
- Sustaining and creating a positive and cooperative political environment in Canada-U.S. defence relations is in Canada's vital interest.
- Canada has a vital interest in preserving the North American Aerospace Defence Command (NORAD) as the basis for a collective approach to North American defence, since NORAD is responsible for monitoring Canadian territory and the United States pays about 92 percent of its operating costs.

The new government initiated talks with the Americans in January 2004 expressly to "negotiate in the coming months a Missile Defence Framework Memorandum of Understanding with the United States with the objective of including Canada as a participant in the current U.S. missile defence program."[4] This initiative had already been supported by a majority in the House of Commons which, in June 2003, passed the following Canadian Alliance motion 156 to 73:

> That this House affirm its strong support for NORAD as a viable defence organisation to counter threats to North America, including the threat of ballistic missile attack; and support giving NORAD responsibility for the command of any system developed to defend North America against ballistic missiles.[5]

Then, in August 2004, Canada agreed to allow NORAD to pass information on ballistic missile threats to the U.S. BMD command. The Canadian policy intent seemed very clear.

Two weeks after the installation of the final phase one missile at Fort Greely, George W. Bush paid his first visit to Canada in nearly four years as president. Although widely interpreted as exerting pressure on Canada, Bush picked up on the Martin government's own initiative when he stated in Halifax that: "I hope we will move forward on ballistic missile defence cooperation to protect the next generations of Canadians and Americans from the threats we know will arise."[6]

The United States did not need Canadian participation to make BMD operational. Nor did it need, or seek, a Canadian financial contribution. It was offering Canada a seat at the table, on design and operational decisions, asking in return only that we offer political support, which the government of Canada had already identified as in our national interest.

On February 22, 2005, Canada made a 180-degree turn. It said no.

Defaulting Control to Washington

The government claimed that its decision was simply the product of a decision to spend Canadian resources on defence matters that were deemed to be a higher priority. However, there was never any indication that a major Canadian financial contribution was being sought.

What Ottawa said no to was the political process that it itself had initiated.[7] In doing so, it forfeited any role in the further development of

BMD. It also abrogated any right to a role in potential launch decisions. In essence, Ottawa signalled Canadian ambivalence to a matter, which in Washington, was perceived as a key issue for the defence of North America.

The implications for the defence relationship are profound. As then-ambassador Paul Cellucci put it, "We simply cannot understand why Canada would, in effect, give up its sovereignty—its seat at the table—to decide what to do about a missile that might be coming toward Canada."[8] Later he added:

> We have this odd situation where the Canadians will participate at NORAD, detecting when the missile is launched, determining where it's heading, and even if they determine it's heading towards Canada, it's at that point they will have to leave the room, because they're not participating.[9]

Soon after the decision was announced, Paul Martin insisted that Canada would have a say in such a decision anyway. But since any launch of an interceptor must be made well within the first few minutes of a missile flight lasting less than 30 minutes in total, his claim was ridiculous.

This about-face was based on domestic political considerations: the Martin government held a minority in the House of Commons, the prime minister was facing dissension within his own Liberal Party, Quebec public opinion was largely opposed to missile defence, and the opposition parties were all either opposed to or vague on BMD.[10] Unprepared to defend, or even explain, the realities of missile defence, or Canadian interests, to any of these groups, the prime minister found it easier to reverse course and abrogate all responsibility to the United States.

Whatever its domestic merits, this decision has significant negative implications for Canada's national security policy. It leaves the United States to take all decisions on missile defence unilaterally. Even if missiles are heading toward Canadian cities, whether deliberately or through error or malfunction, the absence of Canada from the BMD chain of command gives it no say in decisions whether to try to shoot them down. The fact that such a strategic posture could be adopted based on transient domestic political considerations shows how entirely Canada lacks a "strategic culture" that takes national interests seriously.

The broader political repercussions of this decision for Canada are even more unattractive than its immediate strategic consequences. That such a major decision to opt out of BMD could be made in a way so offensive to our main ally, on the basis of such transparently weak excuses, sent the message to Washington that the Canadian government was simply not to be trusted on major defence issues.

An early warning sign was how unusually blunt Americans outside the administration were about it. Dwight Mason, a former American co-chairman of the Canada-U.S. Permanent Joint Board on Defence said: "the basic partnership policy underlying the U.S.-Canadian defence relationship" is now in question.[11] Former U.S. embassy political councillor David Jones warned of "residual resentment" in the United States "that Canadians should be aware of". "There is a point", he added, "as with the shiftless brother-in-law, when you know he will never pull his weight ... Canadians continue to assume that the U.S. will remain benign, and the essential elements of their sovereignty will remain intact."[12] But, he suggested, it might no longer be so. American defence analyst Christopher Sands told an Ottawa audience in March 2005 that Canada's handling of BMD strengthened the views of those in Washington who believe a cooperative approach to bilateral relations should be supplanted by a policy of treating Canada as a protectorate; in effect an object, rather than an independent actor, in North American security.[13] And in his memoirs, former ambassador Paul Cellucci said: "I'm sure that the missile defense decision made by the Canadian government in 2005 is not one that historians will judge to have been in the best interests of Canadian security and sovereignty."[14]

Some Canadians are uncomfortably aware of this fallout. Political scientist Michel Fortmann warned the House of Commons Foreign Affairs Committee in December 2004 that if Canada did not make the effort to participate in North American defence, the United States would simply "take charge of defending Canada as if it were part of their territory". He asked, "Is that what we want? Do we want to become a Liechtenstein or a Principality of Monaco?"[15]

Without knowing it, the former Martin government answered yes to that question. If we are to avoid such a fate, it is imperative that this issue be revisited.

Muddled Strategic Thinking

In recent years, many analysts have referred to the decline in Canadian international "influence." The 2002 edition of the series "Canada Among Nations" referred to Canada as "A Fading Power."[16] The 2003 report "In the National Interest," written by six of the most senior Canadian foreign affairs academics, concluded that "Canada has slipped badly in international influence over the past decade."[17] In *While Canada Slept*, Andrew Cohen argues that Canada has lost "authority" and "direction" in foreign policy.[18] Similarly, in her influential 2004 book, *At Home in the World*, Jennifer Welsh says: "We find ourselves at a crossroads. Either we make the choices that will allow us to thrive on the North American continent and contribute actively in creating a better world, or we will cease to exist—in anything but name—as a sovereign country."[19]

Canadian vulnerability was tacitly acknowledged by Prime Minister Paul Martin in his forward to the Government's 2005 *International Policy Statement*. Martin noted that: "independent countries like Canada—countries with small populations—risk being swept aside, their influence diminished, their ability to compete hampered. This may sound dramatic, but the stakes are that high."[20]

However, "the stakes are that high" because Canada's decline is about much more than a simple loss of influence. And the causes go beyond a general unwillingness to invest in international policy capabilities. As Table 1 shows, it is certainly true that for nearly 40 years, Canadian political leaders have been unwilling to spend what is needed to make us an effective partner in NATO and in North America. But they have been unwilling because they have failed to comprehend the larger and fundamental consequences of failing to do so. It is this penchant for muddled strategic thinking that must be remedied first.

Table 1: Canadian Foreign Aid and Defence Spending as a Percentage of National Wealth (GDP), Selected Years 1962 to 2003–04

	1962-63	1974-75	1984-85	1996-97	2003-04
Foreign Aid	0.13	0.49	0.49	0.3	0.24
Defence	4.5	2.0	2.1	1.2	1

Source: International Institute of Strategic Studies, *Military Balance* (Years 1968 to 2003 inclusive); CIDA, *Canadian Historical Overseas Development Assistance (ODA) System: Statistical Report on ODA, 2002–03*. Figures for 2003–04 from: "CIA World Fact Book": [http://www.cia.gov/cia/publications/factbook/geos/]; Aid as percent of GDP in 2003–04 as reported by the Organization for Economic Cooperation and Development (OECD) [http://www.oecd.org/countrylist/0,2578,en_2649_34485_1783495_1_1_1_1,00.html].

This is a tall order because the "free rider" tradition runs deep in Canadian history. In 1924, Senator Raoul Dandurand described Canada's position in the world as akin to "a fire-proof house, far from inflammable materials." This "sloppy" way of thinking about the nature of the international system, as it was termed by David Frum[21], has been characteristic of the thinking of most of Canada's political leaders since that time.

In January 1991, two days before the outbreak of the first Gulf War, Lloyd Axworthy, then the opposition critic for external affairs, rose to speak in the House of Commons in the hastily called debate on the question of Canada's participation in the coming war. Understandably, he lamented the coming war. But he also emotionally condemned Canada's pending involvement for a unique reason. He believed it would cause our country to lose its "innocence." He described a discussion he had had with a Canadian who, he said, had claimed it would:

> ... no longer be possible for Canadians to see themselves in a world where, by wearing a little maple leaf on our lapel, that we would be seen as the world's Boy Scouts and that we would have open access. All of a sudden, we would have the scales drop from our eyes and we would now see ourselves in a world where there can be ruthless dictators detaining internationals.[22]

Although this comment would likely have baffled Canadian veterans of the Second World War or Korea, the scales never did drop from Mr.

Axworthy's eyes. A varying degree of naiveté has characterized the foreign policies of Canadian governments from John Diefenbaker to Paul Martin and indeed before.

Far too many senior Canadian policy-makers believe influence in foreign policy is grounded more in what one says, and how one says it, than in the capabilities one brings to the table. Such poor understanding of basic power realities in the international system, and a persistent failure to measure its results against those aimed for and anticipated, reflects our weak strategic culture. British strategist Ken Booth defines "strategic culture" as:

> a nation's traditions, values, attitudes, patterns of behaviour, habits, symbols, achievements and particular ways of adapting to the environment and solving problems with respect to the threat or use of force.

It "... is derived from a nation's history, geography and political culture and represents the aggregate of attitudes and patterns of behaviour of the most influential voices in the country."[23] In Canada, "the aggregate of attitudes and patterns of behaviour" related to "the use of force", can be summarized by two words: neglect and indifference.

In 1962, analyst R. J. Sutherland concluded that "Canada has no particular tradition of strategic calculation",[24] while in the 1980s, R.B Byers noted that despite thirty years of Cold War and formal autonomy in international affairs since at least 1931, Canada never developed its own security policy—meaning a strategy for integrating the diplomatic, military, and aid dimensions of policy in a single cohesive framework.[25] Although a rudimentary security policy was finally cobbled together by the government of Paul Martin in April 2004,[26] it is doubtful whether the importance of realistic strategic thinking has yet penetrated deeply into the consciousness of our nation's political, bureaucratic, journalistic, and even academic elites, who have little grasp of strategic or military matters.

In the same month that the national security policy was unveiled, the prime minister, in a major address on military policy, twice referred to the Canadian "invasion of Norway" (he meant Normandy).[27] Just a few months earlier, then-National Defence minister John McCallum, in a letter to a newspaper, confused "Vichy", the French collaborationist government in the Second World War, with "Vimy", the 1917 First World War battle generally agreed to represent Canada's international coming of age. That letter was almost certainly vetted by several officials in his office, yet nobody caught the mistake. A country whose national leaders confuse basic facts about its military history is a country in which limited attention is devoted to strategic matters.

As this tragicomic military ignorance underlines, the crucial weakness in Canada's strategic culture is the failure to pay attention to the issue of power in the international system and how Canada is affected by it and can use it to its advantage. As Denis Stairs put it, in Canada it is assumed that: "Nice states, liberal states, simply did not (certainly it was thought, they *should* not) do that sort of thing."[28] The consequence is a chronic inability to define and effectively advance our national interests.

The "Weak State"

Weak or absent strategic thinking is partly the result of the enduring perception that Canada is "a fire-proof house, far from inflammable materials." But that doesn't explain it entirely. Other states, including the United States and Australia, have also been relatively immune from direct military threats for most of their histories. Yet both have generally had stronger traditions of realistic strategic thinking.

One major difference between Canada and the United States is that here decision making on the most important international policy matters has always been concentrated in the hands of the prime minister and in a relatively small circle of individuals around him. Their approaches to international policy have often been based on their personal, sometimes uninformed, views and inclinations. Most prime ministers (Lester Pearson and to some extent Louis St. Laurent excepted) have had little exposure to international affairs before taking office and rather scattered interest in it thereafter. Over the past decade, Canada's international policy has also become much more ideological and politicized. Neither is conducive to realistic policy making or informed debate of the national interest.

Parliament, with its only elected chamber tightly controlled by the executive branch, is on the outside looking in. This contributes to superficial understanding of key issues on the part of parliamentarians and retards the development of a culture of knowledge and awareness among

MPs (who are also potential future ministers). It inhibits the injection of new ideas and the consideration of other points of view. Most crucially, it severs the link between the Canadian people and those meant to make policy on their behalf.

A weak and detached approach to policy making also means that much of Canada's international policy is driven by inertia and the bureaucratic interests of particular departments. Too often, policy is uncoordinated and reactive. In 2003, a Privy Council Office task force on Canadian international policy concluded that:

> The absence of strong strategic policy direction was the number one concern raised by departments during the Task Force consultations. Without this direction, departments lack a clear vision of Canada's role in the world, its key interests and its policy priorities.[29]

Internal weaknesses in the Canadian state, and the bad policy which it often gives rise to, make it externally weak as well. This carries serious consequences. As Christopher Sands has remarked: "If [Ottawa] continues to adopt a weak country strategy it will fade in its ability to represent and defend Canadian interests in the United States, while fading in its attractiveness as a partner for Washington in the management of cross-border issues."[30]

Certainly there are some instances where Canada has been able to lead, rather than follow, even in terms of Canada-U.S. relations in recent years. For example, Jennifer Welsh has noted that Canada took the lead in drafting the recent "smart border declaration" in negotiations with the United States.[31] But it is harder and harder to do as America's overall confidence in Canada wanes and a lack of any real strategic planning in Ottawa leaves cross-departmental coordination weak, limits long-term policy consistency, and results in policy being largely reactive and ad hoc.

In the absence of such policy effectiveness, it is easy to drift into a policy that is emotionally and politically gratifying, without periodically undertaking a hard-headed evaluation of its effectiveness in the world. But such drifting is harmful to restoring a truly effective bilateral Canadian/American partnership. The alternative then becomes inevitable.

The Implications of Protectorate Status

It is difficult to determine precisely when a smaller state moves from the status of partner of a larger state to that of protectorate—that is, a weak nation under the protection, and indeed partial control, of a stronger state. However, for Canada the process has been underway for some time. Although most Canadians may only be vaguely aware of it, over the past decade Canada's sovereignty has been steadily eroding and Canada is increasingly confronted with ever narrowing policy options.

As will be discussed in chapter three, few states are as vulnerable and dependent on a single economic and security partner as Canada is on the United States. The anchor of Canadian prosperity and security is the relationship with the United States. While it is true that a protectorate relationship would partially secure that prosperity and security, it would also largely eliminate any effective Canadian influence. Only a partnership based on good faith, mutual respect, understanding, and shared decision-making can do that.

However, on BMD Canada has not only signalled that it takes this partnership for granted, it is in fact prepared to see the United States take all the decisions; that it neither wants nor needs any input.

The Canadian decision related to missile defence is only the latest event in decline of the country's influence with its most important ally. Canada's international policy over the past decade has encompassed a fairly long list of initiatives and policies, including such things as the anti-personnel land mines treaty, support for the international criminal court, a comprehensive nuclear test-ban treaty, a pro-Castro policy, the moral condemnation of both the American military campaign in Iraq, which have undermined the Canada-U.S. relationship. To varying degrees, all were perceived as hostile to American interests. What is ironic, of course, is that none were of central importance to Canada's hard interests.

Given the asymmetries in the Canada-U.S. relationship, it is the United States that will determine the nature of the bilateral relationship and the consultations in which it is prepared to engage. Initially at least, while the United States is unlikely to compel Canada to do certain things (such as send troops overseas to support U.S. foreign policy initiatives for example), it may well act more unilaterally when it comes to North American affairs; taking decisions on bilateral issues and simply presenting them to Canada as a *fait accompli*. As this occurs, Canada will be less of a partner in North American affairs and, by default, more of a protectorate.

The former Martin government showed few signs of thinking about how to avoid this predicament. While the Harper government has the opportunity to move in a different direction, it is also up to academics, journalists, and ordinary citizens to lead the way. As the next three chapters will show, a large part of the problem is that policy-makers, of recent years, and those in close orbit around them, have been tightly in the grip of a series of seductive illusions about our role in the world.

— NOTES —

[1] Department of National Defence, *1994 Defence White Paper*, p. 25.

[2] Interview in the *Washington Post*, July 14, 2000 cited by Council for a Livable World, *Statements by Foreign Leaders Opposing National Missile Defense* (February 2001) [see: http://www.armscontrolcenter.org/archives/000326.php].

[3] CTV News online "Rice, Canada to Discuss Missile Shield" (March 1, 2005). Earlier, in April 2003, he was even more specific: "I certainly don't want to see Canada isolated from any moves that the United States might take to protect the continent. If there are going to be missiles that are going off over Canadian airspace, I think that we want to be at the table." Stephen Maher "Missile Defence Flip-Flop Compounds Mr. Dithers Tag" *Halifax Herald* (February 26, 2005).

[4] Exchange of Letters between Defence Minister David Pratt and US Defense Secretary Donald Rumsfeld (January 2004)

[5] House of Commons. *Debates*, May 29 and June 3, 2003

[6] United States. White House. "President Discusses Relationship with Canada" (December 1, 2004)

[7] For a thorough discussion, see: James Fergusson, "Shall We Dance? The Missile Defence Decision, NORAD Renewal, and the Future of Canada-US Relations" *Canadian Military Journal* (Summer 2005): 13–22.

[8] Stephen Maher "Missile Defence Flip-Flop Compounds Mr. Dithers Tag" *Halifax Herald* (February 26, 2005).

[9] CTV News online: "Cellucci Says Canada Reneged on Missile Plan" (March 6, 2005).

[10] While the Conservative Party supported Canadian participation in BMD in

the run-up to the 2004 election, it backed away from open support in the minority parliament.

[11] Alexander Panetta "Canadian Rejection of Missile Defence Historic, Unpredictable Shift: Analysts" Canadian Press, February 25, 2005.

[12] David T. Jones "When Politics Trumps Security: A Washington Vantage Point" *Policy Options* (Montreal: IRPP, May 2005): 49–50.

[13] Christopher Sands, Remarks at the Conference of Defence Associations Annual Meeting, Ottawa, March 3, 2005.

[14] Excerpt from *Unquiet Diplomacy* in *Maclean's* (September 26, 2005).

[15] House of Commons, Standing Committee on Foreign Affairs and International Trade, *Evidence* (December 8, 2004) Testimony at 16:25 Minutes.

[16] Norman Hilmer and Maureen Molot ed., *Canada Among Nations, 2002: A Fading Power* (Oxford University Press, 2002).

[17] Denis Stairs, David Bercuson, Mark Entwistle, J.L. Granatstein, Kim Richard Nossal, Gordon Smith, *In the National Interest: Canadian Foreign Policy in an Insecure World* (Canadian Defence and Foreign Affairs Institute, 2003) p. viii

[18] *While Canada Slept* pp. 23 to 25

[19] Jennifer Welsh, *At Home in the World: Canada's Global Vision for the 21st Century* (Toronto: Harper Collins, 2004) p. 21

[20] Canada. *Canada's International Policy Statement: A Role of Pride and Influence in the World* Overview Paper (2005) "Forward from the Prime Minister"

[21] underground royal commission interview with David Frum (March 27, 2004)

[22] House of Commons, *Debates*, 34th Parliament, 2nd Session, Vol 13. (January 15, 1991) pp. 17026–17027.

[23] Definitions taken from Ken Booth, *Strategy and Ethnocentrism* (New York: Holmes & Meier Publishers, Inc., 1979), p. 121 Alastair Iain Johnston refers to strategic culture as: "[a]An integrated system of symbols (i.e. argumentation structures, languages, analogies, metaphors, etc) that acts to establish pervasive and long-lasting grand strategic preferences by formulating concepts of the role and efficacy of military force in interstate political affairs, and by clothing these conceptions with such an aura of factuality that the strategic preferences seem uniquely realistic and efficacious." Cited by David Haglund, "What Good is Strategic Culture?" *International Journal* LIX (Summer 2004): 485.

[24] R. J. Sutherland, "Canada's Long Term Strategic Situation" *International Journal* 17 (Summer 1962): 199–223.

[25] R. B. Byers, *Canadian Security and Defence: The Legacy and the Challenges* (London: International Institute for Strategic Studies, Winter 1985).

[26] Canada. Privy Council Office, *Securing an Open Society: Canada's National Security Policy* (April 2004).

[27] The speech was given at CFB Gagetown on April 14, 2004. One might explain the reference as a slip of the tongue but for the fact that it happened twice in the same speech.

[28] Denis Stairs, "Hard Choices in Canadian Foreign Policy" in David Carment, Fen Osler Hampson and Norman Hillmer ed., *Canada Among Nations 2004* (Montreal: McGill-Queen's University Press, 2005) p. 23.

[29] Privy Council Office, *Toward an International Policy Framework for the 21st^st Century* (Privy Council Office, July 2003).

[30] See discussion of the weak vs. strong state approach in: Christopher Sands "Fading Power or Rising Power: 11 September and Lessons from the Section 110 Experience" Maureen Appel Molot and Norman Hillmer ed. *Canada Among Nations 2002: A Fading Power* (Toronto: Oxford University Press, 2002) pp. 71–72.

[31] Jennifer Welsh, At Home in the World: Canada's Global Vision for the 21st Century, pp. 58–60.

CHAPTER 2

An Ideological Policy and Its Consequences

like to stand up to the Americans. It's popular.

–Jean Chrétien, former prime minister

In July 1997, Prime Minister Jean Chrétien attended a summit meeting of the North Atlantic Treaty Organization (NATO) in Spain. While speaking with Prime Minister Jean-Luc Dehaene of Belgium, before the meeting began, Mr. Chrétien made some candid comments about American foreign policy. "All the (American) politicians would be in prison ... [in] your country and my country," he stated, because, "they sell their votes." He argued that the expansion of NATO's membership had nothing to do with "world security" and instead was driven by the desire of the Clinton administration to buy votes domestically.[1]

What Chrétien did not realize was that he was speaking into an open mike and that his comments were being picked up by the media. While some might be tempted to dismiss the remarks as the type of chatter that might result from political frustration over this or that issue, they nevertheless expose an anti-American tendency long evident in Canadian international policy. Indeed, Chrétien bluntly indicated that he regarded anti-Americanism as politically useful. "I like to stand up to the Americans. It's popular," he told his Belgian counterpart. He bragged that on the issue of Cuba, for instance, "I was the first one to stand up. And people like that." He did acknowledge, however, that, "you have to be very careful because they're our friends."[2]

This mentality is hardly unique to the former prime minister. Prime Minister Paul Martin played to the same sentiment in his decision to reject a Canadian role in ballistic missile defence. Anti-Americanism was also a prominent theme in the Liberal Party's 2005-06 election campaign. While this may be counterproductive in terms of advancing Canadian interests, Jack Granatstein has noted that Canadian "political and cultural elites continue to use anti-Americanism for their own purposes."[3] In other words, it is particular domestic political objectives that are perceived to be advanced by anti-Americanism. Most Canadian leaders, with the exception of some, such as Brian Mulroney, have viewed Canada-U.S. relations in this context. Regardless of whether Republicans or Democrats have dominated the political scene in the United States, playing an anti-American card has been perceived as generating political payoffs.

That anti-Americanism is seen as politically useful is indicative of something else. It reveals much about what Canadian international policy has become, in a general sense. Instead of being about advancing the national interest, foreign policy is perceived by many politicians as an extension of domestic partisan politics.

In October 2004, then foreign minister Pierre Pettigrew delivered a foreign policy speech in Gatineau, Quebec. In that speech he asserted that Canadian "foreign policy, more than any other area of government activity," expressed "the personality" of the country. Canada's "personality", he argued, encompassed adherence to "common values" such as diversity, multiculturalism, and promoting global "solidarity and balance." He argued that in the new world, as seen from Ottawa at least, "we are well beyond the traditional domain of power politics as played out between states."[4]

Linking this interpretation of "the essence of Canada" explicitly with the government's foreign policy agenda he then warned that, "Stephen Harper's desire to hold a debate about transforming our federalist approach to one based on language and geography ... is precisely the opposite of what we should be doing." Instead, he asserted that: "Canada's hope to have a greater influence on the world stage lies in our values and the importance we place on diversity. It is what makes us truly Canadian ...."[5]

The idea that international influence flows from a narrow and highly partisan interpretation of domestic values is absurd. But to imply that questioning this interpretation is un-Canadian is an attempt to close off all debate on the essence of the country's international policy. Canada's international policy has become highly ideological, mostly reflecting the particular values, beliefs and agendas of those who formulate the policy. Canadian decision-makers themselves have become socialized within myths they themselves have been instrumental in creating.[6] While Canada's international policy is increasingly driven by domestic partisan politics, it is nevertheless cloaked in the language of values.

The Chrétien government's 1995 Foreign Policy White Paper claimed that Canada was in a unique position to promote particular *Canadian values* internationally including "tolerance, the rule of law and thoughtful compromise."[7] A decade later, the Martin government's 2005 International Policy Statement has also put "value" promotion front and centre in charting a course for Canadian foreign policy. This way of thinking has even filtered down to such documents as the 2001 Canadian naval strategy paper *Leadmark,* which asserts that the navy must defend Canadian *values*, not Canadian interests, internationally. These values are said to include:

- Democracy and the rule of law;
- Individual rights and freedoms as articulated in the Canadian Charter of Rights and Freedoms;
- Peace, order and good government as defined in Canada's Constitution; and, Sustainable economic well-being.[8]

The problems inherent in this policy orientation should be self-evident. How can a relatively small state realistically hope to promote such unique values universally and globally? It boggles the mind to believe, for instance, that Canada (let alone the navy specifically) will have any substantive success in promoting so specific a concept such as "peace, order, and good government" when that concept is unique to Canada's particular constitutional history and culture.

This chapter examines the increasingly grandiose objectives that have characterized Canadian international policy as well as the ideology that has given rise to them. It analyzes and questions both the political motivations underscoring this policy approach and the idea that unique Canadian values must serve as the primary basis for the country's international policy. It seeks to illustrate that such an approach to international policy is not only unrealistic, it runs counter to Canadian interests. Moreover, the inherent anti-Americanism that it gives rise to has slowly eroded the country's vital partnership with the United States.

Fire and Ice?

Recently, Canada's leading liberal international affairs thinker (and now Liberal MP), Michael Ignatieff, argued that: "Maintaining our national independence is our guiding national interest ...."[9] Like so many other Canadians, he principally means maintaining our independence from the United States. But what does this mean in a continent that is as economically integrated as North America? And what relevance does such a statement have in the context of two societies that are as culturally similar as those of Canada and the United States?

For many states, the maintenance of national independence is indeed the overarching imperative of international policy. Certainly this is the case when the value systems of potential neighbours and adversaries are alien or hostile to one's own values. Regardless of cultural similarities, South Korea has a strong interest in maintaining complete independence from North Korea, so long as the latter state continues to pose a fundamental threat to South Korea's values and way of life. The same might be said of the relationship between Taiwan and communist China for example. But within the Western community of states, common democratic values and increasing economic integration have diluted the meaning of absolute national independence. This is the case both in Europe and in North America.

That many Canadians continue to think in terms of the importance of maintaining absolute national independence is partly a product of history. English Canada's early identity was based on a rejection of the revolutionary ideas found in the United States. The United Empire Loyalists came to Canada precisely because they rejected the ideas of the American Revolution. Subsequent experiences, such as American invasion during the War of 1812, and Canada's continuing loyalty to the British Empire, reinforced that early tradition.

However, while the early history of Canadian-U.S. relations was often characterized by hostility, the history of the past 135 years has been entirely peaceful. Indeed, during the 20th century, the two countries have grown together, not only in economic, military, and political terms, but also in a cultural sense. These growing connections rest on a bedrock of common values and an instinctive mutual understanding.

Yet for many Canadians, the idea that the United States constitutes a threat to Canada is not part of history. Instead, they believe that the nature of American society, coupled with that country's strength, constitutes a kind of existential threat to Canada and its alleged values.

"Increasingly different" Canadian and American values is the central thesis of the book by Michael Adams. Based on the results of opinion surveys in both countries over the past decade, Adams asserts that a far greater percentage of Canadians than Americans tend toward notions of "idealism and autonomy" in terms of how they see the world and their place in it.[10] This, he argues, has a profound effect on social and political attitudes. Thomas Axworthy agrees, arguing that Canadians, like Europeans, "hold to a multicultural, social democratic pluralist ethic, while Americans increasingly are retrenching into an exclusionary, competitive world view."[11]

Other thinkers have also stressed the differences that exist between Canadian and American political culture. These are seen to be the product not only of differing political systems, but also unique historical experiences. Canada's remarkably peaceful historical evolution is often contrasted with that of the United States. So too is the existence of the "French fact" in Canadian history. The two combined are said to have engendered a "spirit of compromise" in Canada's national character, which makes the country fundamentally different from the United States. In this regard, John Ralston Saul has quoted Robert Baldwin's description of the "art of Canadian compromise" as:

> ... that forbearance, moderation and firmness on the part of the people which, so long as it compromises no great principle, affords the best assurance of the possession of fitness for the exercise of political power.[12]

Michael Adams argues that distinct political cultures manifest themselves in differing attitudes toward violence and the use of force in the two countries. In this regard, he cites one poll from 2000, which found that nearly a third of Americans thought that "a little violence" was "no big deal", whereas only 14 percent of Canadians agreed with that proposition. Nevertheless, as Adams himself acknowledges, in 1992, exactly the same number of Canadian as American respondents supported that same assertion. No explanation is given as to why results might be so different just eight years apart.[13]

Illustrating what he regards as fundamental attitudinal differences, Mr. Adams also argues, for instance, that after the events of September 11, 2001, Canadians "found themselves beginning to roll their eyes at phrases like 'axis of evil'."[14] But what is forgotten is that the oft-quoted phrase apparently originated with a Canadian—David Frum—then a speechwriter for President Bush. And while perhaps Mr. Adam's friends "rolled their eyes" at the phrase, many other Canadians did not.

It is largely poll results, capturing the political mood at particular moments in time, that are used to try to substantiate assertions that Canadians have very different attitudes from Americans and that on international issues, the two countries are "growing apart." Among such surveys are an Ipsos-Reid survey in 2005 found that the numbers of Canadians regarding the U.S. as the country's "closest ally" had fallen from 60 percent in 2002 to 53 percent in 2005.[15] Similarly, at the time of the Iraq war, a CRIC poll found that while 46 percent of Americans believed that it would be "possible to disarm Iraq using peaceful means", 67 percent of Canadians agreed with that notion. Forty-four percent of Americans and 32 percent of Canadians disagreed with that assertion.

But while such results may suggest that from time-to-time Canadian attitudes toward the United States fluctuate, or that Canadians might have slightly different perspectives on certain international issues, it is questionable whether they indicate much more than that. With respect to Iraq, a Leger Marketing poll from January 2003 found that while going to war over Iraq was not popular, 44 percent of Canadians nevertheless believed that Canada should stand by the United States if military action went ahead (43 percent were opposed). The numbers who believed in standing with the United States rose to 48.5 percent in English Canada (with 36.5 percent opposed) but fell to 30 percent in Quebec (with 62 percent opposed).[16]

Less supportive numbers in support of military action in Iraq might have had less to do with Canadian "principles" or the absence of UN political sanction than the fact that Canadian troops were not deployed in the field. Had they been, and had the government taken a position similar to that of Great Britain or Australia, Canadian poll results might have been very different.

Indeed, what is clear from polling is that whenever Canada has participated in conflict, since 1989, Canadians have tended to be supportive whether the war has been sanctioned by the United Nations or not. For example, 72 percent of Canadians supported Canadian involvement in the bombing of Serbia in 1999, a war that was not sanctioned by the UN Security Council. Support declined somewhat as the war went on, but it never slipped below 50 percent.[17] American support for the war in Kosovo was slightly less than that in Canada, also oscillating between 53 and 62 percent.[18] In 2002, Canadian support for military involvement in Afghanistan lagged only slightly behind that in the United States—75 percent vs. 88 percent.[19]

In contrast to various polls that show Canadians and Americans are growing apart, Carleton University Professor Michael Hart has catalogued many poll results that indicate exactly the opposite; that there is a close convergence between Canadian and American attitudes and views of the world. For instance, in some polls of recent years, 75 percent of Canadians supported closer social and cultural relations with the United States, 90 percent favoured closer economic ties, and 60 percent supported ballistic missile defence.[20]

Polls are snapshots of the political mood at particular times. Much depends on who is asked, what they are asked, and when. Within North America, regional differences matter as much as Canadian and American ones. For instance, do North Dakotans share closer values with Manitobans or with people from Mississippi? Is it likely that social attitudes in Alberta will be closer to those in Montana or to those in Quebec? Poll questions that blur such distinct categories and present transient moods as deep-seated national convictions are usually of dubious value.[21]

The different perspectives of Quebecers on political issues are often used as a rationale for distancing Canada from the United States. Yet, as historian Jack Granatstein has pointed out, Quebecers have the same strategic and economic interests at stake in the Canada-U.S. relationship as any other Canadian.[22] What is evident from poll results is that the more Canadians in any part of the country perceive they have major interests at stake on a given issue, the more united national opinion tends to become. This seems to account for poll results, such as those that suggest that up to 90 percent of Canadians are willing to entertain closer economic ties with the United States as well as for the strong national support shown for Canadian troops when committed overseas.

Despite some obvious nuanced differences between Canadian and American societies and values, at a fundamental level our two countries are probably closer than any two countries on earth, including within the European Union (EU) or the British Commonwealth. Looking at sociological studies (for instance, a study released in 2005 by the U.S. National Institute on Aging found that "Canadians and Americans have almost identical personality traits"[23]), work patterns, and other indications of people's real culture—such as taste in popular music, movies, and the like—one is hard-put to find any two other peoples that are closer than Canadians and Americans.

Common Foundational Values and Common Interests

Cultural and societal similarities between Canada and the United States are not a new phenomenon. At the time of the First World War, one Canadian jurist, when comparing Canadians and Americans, commented that:

> An American feels himself at home at once in Canada, a Canadian crossing the border does not feel that he is entering a foreign or strange land; neither can notice any difference in the language or in the habits of the people. Once he escapes the custom-house either feels himself a native—unless he is a fool either by nature or through misplaced or spurious patriotism.[24]

A few years later, Prime Minister Mackenzie King told the Imperial Conference in London that:

> In the settlement of differences between the United States and Canada, we have the inestimable advantage of speaking (for the most part) the same language, and that not merely in the linguistic sense, for we have, in larger measure than is the case in Continental Europe, the same values, the same standards, in part the same traditions.[25]

Along the same lines, President Harry S Truman told Parliament in 1947 that:

> The word 'foreign' [in Canada-U.S. relations] seems strangely out of place. Canada and the United States have reached the point where we no longer think of each other as foreign countries. We think of each other as friends ... The example of accord provided

by our two countries did not come about merely through the happy circumstance of geography. It is compounded by one part proximity and nine parts good will and common sense.[26]

These strong connections, already regarded as self-evident nearly 60 and indeed more than 80 years ago, are certainly no weaker today given the revolution in communications that has occurred in the interim. American James Bennett has written extensively on the "Anglosphere challenge" and about the common cultural values that are shared at a deeper level between the English-speaking democracies. These encompass a "common cultural narrative" stretching back to Magna Carta. They not only encompass a common constitutional and political tradition, but also a similar "intellectual understanding" about the essence and nature of a successful market economy and a strong civil society.[27]

What this means is that the same core values and principles inform both Canadian and American international policy. For instance, the Canadian government has made the "Responsibility to Protect" Agenda the basis of its international policy in the coming decade. A comparison of the values that underscore this agenda with those in the American National Security Strategy of 2002 (see Table 2), suggests that the value motivations in Canadian and American policies are quite similar. It is largely the tactics and the means that differ. This accrues from the power differences between two states. While the United States possesses the means to implement its policy objectives directly, often unilaterally, Canada generally does not.

Common foundational values are cemented by common strategic and economic interests. In 2003, an internal paper produced by the Directorate of Strategic Analysis in the Department of National Defence argued that despite political and tactical differences that existed between American and West Europe or Canadian policies, in the final analysis, "... the strategic interests *and values* of the U.S. and its allies [are] virtually identical" [emphasis added].[28] If that is generally the case for the United States and its allies, it is even more true for Canada and the United States. The integrated nature of the North American economy and the strategic unity of North America means that, on most issues, Canada and the United States naturally share the same interests in terms of their interaction with the rest of the world.

Table 2: Canada's Responsibility to Protect Agenda Compared with the American National Security Strategy

Canada—"Responsibility to Protect" Agenda as Outlined in the International Policy Statement, 2005 *	United States—Corresponding Objectives in the National Security Strategy of the United States, 2002‡
1. Responsibility to Protect, to hold governments accountable for how they treat their people and to intervene, if necessary, to prevent a humanitarian catastrophe.	Freedom is the non-negotiable demand of human dignity; the birthright of every person—in every civilization .... The United States must defend liberty and justice because these principles are right and true for people everywhere. No nation owns these aspirations, and no nation is exempt from them.... We will champion the cause of human dignity and oppose those who resist it.
2. Responsibility to Deny, to prevent terrorists and irresponsible governments from acquiring weapons of mass destruction that could destroy millions of innocent people.	We must be prepared to stop rogue states and their terrorist clients before they are able to threaten or use weapons of mass destruction against the United States and our allies and friends.
3. Responsibility to Respect, to build lives of freedom for all people, based on the fundamental human rights of every man woman and child on earth.	America must stand firmly for the nonnegotiable demands of human dignity; the rule of law; limits on the absolute power of the state; free speech; freedom of worship; equal justice; respect for women; religious and ethnic tolerance; and respect for private property.
4. Responsibility to Build, to make sure our economic assistance programs provide the tools that ordinary people really need to get on with their own development.	A world in which some live in comfort and plenty, while half of the human race lives on less than $2 a day, is neither just nor stable. Including all of the world's poor in an expanding circle of development—and opportunity—is a moral imperative and one of the top priorities of U.S. international policy.
5. Responsibility to the Future, to ensure sustainable development for future generations through better management of global public goods.	The United States must foster economic growth in ways that will provide a better life along with widening prosperity. We will incorporate labor and environmental concerns into U.S. trade negotiations, creating a healthy 'network' between multilateral environmental agreements with the World Trade Organization ...

International Policy Statement, Diplomatic Paper, (2005) p. 20;
‡United States, *The National Security Strategy of the United States of America* (September 2002) pp. vi; 3, 4, 14, 19 and 21

While the existence of two states in North America means that, at times, different tactical policy objectives may be pursued by Washington or Ottawa, the notion that there are fundamental strategic or value-based differences between Canada and the United States is false. It is the product of an ideological approach to international policy in Canada that has driven an artificial wedge between Canada and the United States.

Canada as a Bastion of Moral Virtue?

Despite the similarities between Canadian and American values and interests, much of the Canadian elite nevertheless believes that its values are fundamentally different from those of their American counterparts. While this policy has deep roots, this perception has grown since the election of George W. Bush as president in the United States.

Former Canadian deputy minister of foreign affairs Gordon Smith recently wrote that he believed Michael Adams' thesis, with respect to fundamental differences between Canadian and American values, to be "accurate" based in part on the direction that U.S. foreign policy has taken in recent years. "Canadians see the United States as becoming increasingly unilateralist", he said.

> ... Canadians, and many Europeans, did not like the way the United States dealt with Iraq. The swaggering style of George W. Bush also continues to aggravate seriously the negative perception of US policies in the eyes of many Canadians.[29]

Many have gone much further. In an article in March of 2005, former foreign minister Lloyd Axworthy argued that members of the Bush administration needed to "learn a thing or two" from Canadian values. He argued that unlike in the United States, where massive tax breaks were given to the top one percent of the population "while cutting food programs for poor children", Canada was governed by a "different set of priorities." Internationally, he argued, this manifested itself in a foreign policy that protected the rights of people, not just nation-states. The United States was of course said to be doing exactly the opposite. "There are times", he said "when truth" [meaning Canada] "must speak to power" [meaning the United States].[30]

Obviously, official government statements do not refer to Canada as truth incarnate. Yet this general attitude has come to underscore much of Canada's international policy. At the heart of this is the belief that Canada is not only different from that of the United States, but morally superior.

In the end, it is the wrong way to approach international policy and our relationship with the United States. While ordinary Canadians have the luxury of disliking and protesting the way in which the United States dealt with Iraq or with this or that aspect of the foreign policy of the Bush administration, the foreign policy of the Canadian government should never be sidetracked by emotion. A position based on presumed moral superiority does nothing to advance the interests of the Canadian people. Instead, it has eroded the Canada-U.S. partnership. In November 2005, U.S. ambassador David Wilkins told a Toronto audience that:

> If you listen to some of the rhetoric out there it's like the greatest enemy we face is each other. I believe this is a toxic attitude—one that will impact our relationship if we don't make a concerted effort to build each other up and accentuate the positive.[31]

A public statement of this kind from a serving U.S. ambassador should raise alarm bells in Canada.

We must also recognize that such an approach to international policy is inevitably hypocritical. No state is a bastion of moral virtue. If Canada, in general, seems to pursue a more altruistic international policy than the United States, it is only because we have been shielded from the most unpleasant aspects of international affairs by the United States. This is what allowed our former foreign minister to naively assert that "we are well beyond the traditional domain of power politics as played out between states." Because we do not have the international responsibilities that accrue from superpower status, we have come to believe that we possess a more virtuous national character.

Yet we have conveniently forgotten that, even at our own level, we have often failed to live up to our rhetoric. In recent years, for instance, Canada has chosen to aggressively promote trade with states like China and Cuba, even to protect the interests of one relatively small company in Sudan, while largely pushing human rights concerns into the background. Canada is far from being as virtuous as it pretends.

Despite the contradictions, an ideological approach has continued to serve as the basis for Canada's international policy. This is particularly true of our diplomatic initiatives of recent years. But the gains have been small. And instead of enhancing our reputation and influence where it most matters, they have simply betrayed the growing weakness of Canadian foreign policy.

"Words are the only weapon that the Athenians have left" *

The idea that Canada is, and must be, a kind of model power in the international system has become a poor man's ideological international policy. During his trip to Asia early in 2005, Prime Minister Paul Martin commented that: "I believe that we have built one of the strongest countries in the world and certainly a country that the rest of the world can use as a model."[32]

Yet the absence of resources to support foreign policy is an obvious problem. Lloyd Axworthy attempted to solve this by developing a uniquely Canadian interpretation of the concept of "soft power." According to Mr. Axworthy, Canada was "well placed to succeed as a leader in a world where soft power is increasingly important."[33] In his conception, soft power "blurs, even counters, the perception of traditional power assets, such as military force, economic might, resources, and population. Power in this context is obtained from networking and coalition-building."[34]

Policy that is ideologically driven is often detached from reality. Since the Axworthy years there has been a grudging realization, in some circles at least, that power indeed matters. Capabilities supporting credible policy, rather than rhetoric, are the real basis of international influence.

The Martin government's International Policy Statement (IPS) of April 2005 promised to back up the model approach with more resources. But the very notion that Canada is a model power remains highly questionable. For instance, the IPS, which was rushed out in anticipation of a possible spring 2005 federal election (which in the end did not occur), argues that:

---

* Sarcastic Roman reference to Athens rhetorical support for Rome's war against Macedonia, 2nd Century B.C. cited by Tom Holland, *Rubicon: The Last Years of the Roman Republic* (New York: Anchor Books, 2005) p. 76

For those countries where violence threatens to overtake political accommodation as the answer to competing interests,
Canada's long history of accommodation of linguistic, ethnic
and cultural differences—dating from the Quebec Act of 1774—
offers a glimmer of hope. Our system of governance represents a
laboratory full of intriguing experiments that can assist others
engaged in the complex task of institution building. This understanding of the 'DNA' of governance is an important resource
that Canada can use to make a difference.[35]

It is true that Canada's history is unique, as is its constitutional and
political path. However, to imply that Canada understands the "'DNA' of
governance" across societies and cultures, is simplistic. And the notion
that a particular (and very recent) interpretation of Canadian history should
serve as a guide for the priorities of contemporary Canadian international
policy is a dubious foundation for the foreign policy of a small state.

Despite obvious shortcomings, this approach has generated significant
support in Canada's academic community. Michael Ignatieff argues that
Canada has a key role to play in exporting the values of peace, order, and
good government to the world.[36] Jennifer Welsh, who was briefly hired
by the Martin government in 2005 to help draft the International Policy
Statement, made positioning Canada as a "model citizen" in the international community a central feature in her widely referenced book on
Canadian policy. "I propose a simple but ambitious vision for Canada's
global role: as Model Citizen", she wrote. She agreed with the viewpoint
that Canada's civil society and values "are exceedingly attractive" internationally. Canada could, she argued, "demonstrate how to establish the foundations of a strong society—much as a teacher or consultant might do."[37]

Canada25, a group of young Canadians supported by the Department
of Foreign Affairs and other organizations, also made the model power
idea the central feature of their study released in 2004. "We propose that
Canada become a model power—a country whose influence is linked to
its ability to innovate, experiment and partner; a country that, by presenting itself as a model, invites the world to assess, challenge, borrow
from, and contribute to, its efforts."[38]

The essential problem is that the "model approach" to Canadian foreign policy is built on at least two questionable premises. One premise is
that other countries are waiting for advice from Canada with respect to

how to order their societies, safeguard rights, run elections, and write Canadian-style constitutions; that this is the essential source of Canadian influence. This is not to say that Canada does not possess certain national assets that may enhance its role in particular regions or countries at particular times. For instance, Canada's large ethnic Ukrainian community afforded the country with the opportunity of playing an enhanced role in Ukraine's transition to democracy. Yet in the final analysis, there is no basis on which to argue that Canada's domestic political model is a more attractive model than that of United States, Scandinavian countries or, indeed, any other European state. Neither is there any reason to believe that this approach will enhance Canada's influence in a way that actually advances the interests of ordinary Canadians.

The second questionable premise is that Canadian governments have the will to spend resources commensurate with the aspiration to be a "model power." The Canadian willingness to pursue a truly altruistic values-based foreign and security policy has been largely rhetorical. A real strategy to lead in the rebuilding of failed and failing states, as outlined in the IPS, would require a massive resource commitment, the like of which Canada has not made in international affairs since the 1950s. It would also require policy focus and real knowledge and understanding of global and regional political problems. This would have to be based on country-specific expertise as well as good and informed intelligence. Yet Canada has no foreign intelligence service and the IPS of 2005 did not propose to establish one. The goals of the IPS are, in the end, rhetorical fantasy and not accomplished fact. This outcome does not serve Canada's interests and serves simply to erode its credibility.

Symbolism for Its Own Sake

Inherent in the model approach to foreign policy is the notion that symbolism itself can change the nature of international discourse. In 2000, in a speech in Washington D.C., then foreign minister Lloyd Axworthy argued that: "The language of international affairs has begun to change. This shift in language reflects a change in perception—a recognition that the needs of individuals must be our principal concern. We arrived at this point via the broader realization that there is a changing world reality."[39]

Canada has pursued several diplomatic initiatives over the past decade including: a Comprehensive Test Ban Treaty (CTBT) for nuclear weapons, the anti-personnel land mines treaty, the formation of an International Criminal Court (ICC), and the Kyoto treaty.

However, in each of these areas serious questions exist with respect to the value of the agreements reached. Instead of having the impact that proponents have claimed, they have either been largely ineffective or have actually set back international cooperation. A common dimension to each of them is their failure to garner American support. Indeed, all have come to be perceived in Washington as generally hostile to American interests. In each case, the Canadian government has either known this in advance or has continued to pursue the issue long after it became apparent that the goals have been largely unachievable.

The Comprehensive Test Ban Treaty (CTBT): The CTBT, which was opened for signature to the world's states in 1996, is an outgrowth of an aspiration that emerged in the 1950s to ban all nuclear testing with the eventual aim of ridding the world of all nuclear weapons. While universal nuclear disarmament has always been unlikely, the world's existing nuclear powers did make a nominal commitment in Nuclear Non-Proliferation Treaty (NPT) of 1968 to work toward "a Treaty on general and complete [nuclear] disarmament under strict and effective international control."[40]

Idealists generally believed that the way to begin to achieve this lofty goal was through a comprehensive treaty to ban all nuclear testing. Indeed, the Canadian government has advocated such an agreement since the 1960s. After the end of the Cold War, the goal of such a treaty appeared to be within reach and in 1996 the text of the CTBT was agreed to and declared open for signature. The United States was the first country to sign the treaty.

However, in 1998 the limited value of the CTBT became apparent as India and Pakistan crossed the nuclear threshold with a series of nuclear weapon tests. The Clinton administration still tried to sell the CTBT domestically by arguing that the United States could continue to develop and modernize its nuclear arsenal through "simulated testing" technology, which was becoming increasingly sophisticated. Despite the fact that the United States has not needed to conduct a live nuclear weapon test for years, opponents in Congress worried that a complete ban on testing might possibly hamper future nuclear weapon modernization requirements. The result was that when the agreement finally came before the

U.S. Senate in 1999, the consent required to ratify the treaty was denied. American support then evaporated completely with the election of the Bush administration in 2000.

The CTBT is now effectively dead in the United States. Ratification by 44 designated "nuclear capable" countries is required to bring the treaty into effect, but only 33 have done so. Most of these remaining 11 countries seem unlikely to proceed. This will certainly continue until simulation technology has progressed to the point where actual tests are universally judged to be superfluous to nuclear weapon modernization. At that point, the CTBT may be revived, but it will be strategically irrelevant.

Despite this history, Canada's strong advocacy for the CTBT continues. This could be written off as simple policy inertia were it not for the fact that the underlying and public rationale for Canadian policy is that: "Canada would like to ensure that the CTBT contributes to the ultimate eradication of all nuclear weapons."[41]

The pursuit of this policy is indicative of several things: First, of an inability to differentiate between what, in the minds of some, may be desirable and what is actually achievable. There appears to be no recognition in Canadian government circles that while existing nuclear weapon countries may give lip service to the idea of eradicating nuclear weapons most will never trade the security afforded by their nuclear arsenals in exchange for a paper treaty, no matter how well enforced it may be. It is impossible to imagine, for instance, that the United States would be willing to eliminate its nuclear arsenal, making the world safe for major conventional warfare again, and rely on a treaty instead to provide its security. It is equally difficult to imagine many other countries, Israel to name one, doing the same.

Second, it is indicative of the primacy of domestic politics in Canadian foreign policy. Advocacy of the CTBT enables the government to pretend that it is at the forefront of nuclear arms control efforts. Most people are probably unaware of the fact that the CTBT will not prevent further nuclear weapon modernization. Nor do they give a great deal of consideration to the practical impediments that exist in the path of the eradication of all nuclear weapons. Yet, for the most part, the government rarely has to explain or discuss those issues. Indeed, opposition members of parliament are much more likely to ask why the government isn't doing *more* to eradicate nuclear weapons rather than pointing to the pointlessness of the policy.

Lastly, the policy is illustrative of an inability to judge where Canada's real interests lie. At a UN meeting in New York in 2001 for instance, and only one month after the attacks of 9/11, Canada argued that its "first priority" in international security in the coming year was nuclear disarmament[42]—an absolutely ridiculous goal in the context of world events at the time. The devotion of scarce diplomatic resources to goals that cannot be achieved, and that cost the country credibility with its most important allies, is indicative of a policy that has lost its way.

The Anti-Personnel Landmines Treaty: In 1996, soon after Lloyd Axworthy became foreign minister, Canada decided to support a campaign to conclude a treaty banning the production, use, and trade in anti-personnel landmines. The campaign to conclude such a sweeping treaty came in response to the fact that anti-personnel landmines planted in third-world countries have continued to claim lives for years and even decades after conflicts have ended.

While no one would quarrel with the campaign's objective of cleaning-up the problem of the indiscriminate planting of landmines in the third world, it is less than clear that the treaty promoted by Canada, which, on paper, bans these weapons completely, is an effective way of dealing with the indiscriminant use of anti-personnel landmines. In this regard, two shortcomings of the so-called Ottawa process were evident from the very beginning.

For one, there is little evidence that either rogue or failed countries or militant guerrilla groups are in the slightest way restricted by the treaty signed in Ottawa in December 1997. It is such countries or groups that are principally responsible for the indiscriminate use of landmines around the world.

While the group "Mines Action Canada" claims that mine use is declining, it nevertheless acknowledges that, despite the treaty, 11 armed opposition groups in various parts of the world have used anti-personnel landmines since May, 2002.[43] Some countries that have signed the treaty, such as Angola, have also already violated its terms, leading two analysts to comment: "failure of this landmark international event (the landmines treaty) bodes ill for other nascent forms of arms control, including proscription of the trade in small arms."[44]

Second, a number of countries that require anti-personnel landmines for their security have refused to sign the treaty. These include Israel, South Korea, Finland, the United States, and 38 other countries. The United States made it clear from the outset that it had to look to the security of its forces in South Korea and could not replace anti-personnel mines along the border with North Korea with new technologies until at least 2006. The Clinton administration also informed Canada that while it could support a partial ban on mines that were not self-deactivating, it wanted to retain the option of deploying self-deactivating high tech mines with its forces.

This objective should have created the basis for an acceptable compromise. The primary objective after all was a humanitarian one—to try to establish the conditions in which those mines that were the cause of so many civilian deaths in conflict zones in the third world could be gradually controlled and eventually eliminated. However, for Minister Axworthy and the Canadian government there was to be no compromise. The objective had become one of banning all landmines, regardless of whether they contributed to the problem or not. In an address in New York six months after the treaty was concluded, Mr. Axworthy stated that the compromise proposed by the United States had been "disturbing." He said, that it continued "to cast the problem as a military one" and that it was "part of America's global responsibility to recognize that the world has changed, and that the old ways of doing business no longer hold."[45]

Bent on an ideological approach to the entire problem, Canada has inadvertently ended up making the landmines convention a kind of moral test of *American* foreign policy. It was an approach that was shortsighted because it drove the major players from the negotiating table. Without the political weight of the United States (and two other permanent Security Council members—China and Russia) behind it, the anti-personnel landmines convention has largely become an empty shell.

The International Criminal Court (ICC): The International Criminal Court came into existence in 2002, as a tribunal to prosecute individuals for genocide, war crimes, and crimes against humanity. While nearly 100 countries have acceded to the ICC, the remaining 90 countries of the world have not. Among the latter are three permanent members of the Security Council—the United States, Russia, and China.

On the surface, it may appear to many that the establishment of an international court to try the world's worst war criminals would easily garner nearly universal support. But it has not. Some argue that the ICC is unnecessary; that temporary and ad hoc tribunals, such as those created for the former Yugoslavia or Rwanda, can fulfill the function of the ICC.

However, the more fundamental case made by opponents to the ICC is that the Court could become a forum for politically motivated investigations and prosecutions of elected leaders and of serving soldiers. Since any country that is party to the treaty can initiate a case, and since the crime of "aggression" is left undefined, the resolution of cases is held hostage to the vagaries of the political balance prevailing on the court at any given time.

As constituted, the ICC could potentially stand in judgment over decisions taken by elected governments acting in their national interest. This is an attack on fundamental responsibilities and sovereignty that the United States has been unable to accept. As a result, both the Clinton and George W. Bush administrations, as well as a majority in Congress, have strongly opposed the Court.[46]

In recent years, certain governments have questioned the legality of American and Western military campaigns in Iraq and Kosovo, both of which were undertaken without formal sanction by the United Nations Security Council. This has intensified American concerns with respect to the ICC to the point where the United States has threatened to use its veto to block the renewal of UN peacekeeping mandates unless U.S. servicemen are permanently exempted from the Court's jurisdiction. Congress also passed a *Service-members' Protection Act* in 2002 that prevents American cooperation with the Court and provides for the termination of U.S. military and economic aid to any country that ratified the ICC (NATO members are exempted). By June 2005, about 100 countries had signed bilateral agreements (some in secret) with the United States agreeing not to surrender U.S. nationals to the jurisdiction of the Court.

Canada should share these American concerns for several reasons. First, the support of the United States is central to the establishment of any effective new international legal regime such as that required by the ICC. By itself, an international court without the United States is in an institution of dubious value. But given the depth and vehemence of American opposition, the ICC is likely to be completely ineffective. Common sense dictates that Canada should work towards an effective, rather than an ineffective, court.

Second, Canada has itself participated in recent military campaigns that were not sanctioned by the UN Security Council. In Kosovo, that participation included the commitment of CF-18 fighter aircraft; in Iraq, after 2003, it included Canadian military personnel seconded to serve with American and British forces there. Canadian personnel might themselves become subject to harassing investigations, perhaps prosecution, initiated by any state hostile to Canadian/Western interests.

Third, Canada should recognize, as nearly 100 other countries have done, that its interests do not lie in creating diplomatic and political problems for the United States. A useful model in this regard is Israel. The Israeli position on the ICC has corresponded closely to that of the United States. This concurrence flows from a recognition that demonstrating diplomatic support on an issue of prime importance to the United States is in Israel's long-term interests.

Such an approach to foreign policy is the polar opposite to the one that drives Canadian diplomatic policy. Canada approaches diplomatic issues ideologically; on the basis of what Canadian politicians ideally hope for, rather than on the basis of what the national interest requires or what is realistically achievable. This approach has undermined the country's influence with its most important allies and ultimately serves to undercut many of the broader "human security" goals that Canada has declared it wants to achieve.

The Kyoto Treaty: The most costly of the symbolic agreements that Canada has adhered to in recent years is the Kyoto Accord. This accord was negotiated in 1997 and came into force in 2005. It nominally commits the parties to reducing their "green house gas" emissions by 5.2 percent below 1990 levels by the period 2008–12. Canada is committed to reducing green house gas emissions by 6 percent in that period. In 2005, the Liberal government pledged nearly $10 billion toward anti-green house gas initiatives by 2010.[47]

That environmental issues are important is not in question. There are, however, serious questions as to whether Kyoto is an effective means for addressing the specific problem of green house gas emissions because the reduction targets set out in the accord may well be unachievable. Canada itself has no clear plan for reaching its reduction targets and its own emissions have continued to increase in recent years.[48] Key countries, such as China, India, and Brazil have not been assigned any reduction targets at all. Indeed, it is projected that China alone will probably increase emissions that will easily offset any reductions that may be made elsewhere.[49] This has led even supporters to argue that the treaty's "greatest value is symbolic".[50]

A further weakness with the Kyoto Accord lies in the fact that the United States is not a party to it. This is a crucial factor for Canada given the importance of maintaining economic and trade competitiveness with the United States. Some, such as the Canadian Manufacturers and Exporters Association have warned that "implementing the Kyoto protocol would have a severely damaging effect on Canada's energy and manufacturing sectors." They estimate that were Canada to take the steps necessary to meet its targets, 450,000 jobs would be lost in the manufacturing sector alone.[51]

The treaty sets out a most dubious alternative to meeting reduction targets by permitting "credit purchasing." This allows industrialized countries to "buy" energy reduction "credits" from less developed countries (such as Russia or Mexico) to avoid a situation where they would otherwise fail to meet Kyoto targets. The idea is that wealthier countries unable to meet their own targets can at least help to fund environmental cleanup in less developed countries. Many, however, have questioned who actually will participate in such transactions and whether real environmental cleanup will be the result. For instance, in 2002 Liberal MP John McKay told the House of Commons that he believed that "the likelihood is that we will be buying our credits from the Russian mafia to meet our Kyoto requirements".[52]

The fact that the Kyoto process is a United Nations' process has certainly been a key factor in underscoring Canada's commitment to a dubious endeavour. This fact has reinforced the desire to remain within the Kyoto "consensus", regardless of whether it is working or not. Once again, ideology was a primary policy determinant rather than a dispassionate assessment of the actual effectiveness of the protocol or its potential costs. What is unique about Kyoto, however, are the staggering financial costs to taxpayers. While the CTBT, the land mines treaty (exclusive of mine clean up costs which are a separate issue largely unconnected to the treaty) and the ICC processes may only have cost a few dozen million, Kyoto will end up costing Canadians billions for very little return.

The Irresponsibility of the Ideological Approach

The major Canadian diplomatic policy initiatives of the past decade have placed symbolism over substance. They have done so based on a false belief that Canadian policy approaches to international affairs are morally superior to those of the United States; that these flow from superior Canadian values.

Recently, a former Canadian ambassador to the United Nations, Paul Heinbecker, wrote that part of Canada's role in international affairs is to "interpret" America to the rest of the world and vice versa. Canada must always be prepared to stand up to the United States and, he says, "speak 'truth to power' in Washington. This means":

> not shrinking from dealing frankly, albeit courteously, with U.S. administrations when we think they are wrong, as many Canadians believe they were on issues as diverse as Iraq, the International Criminal Court, Kyoto, and the development of still another generation of nuclear weapons and missile systems.[53]

However, there is considerable self-delusion and, frankly, a degree of hypocrisy in this statement and attitude. Supporting Kyoto is morally "right" even though it will likely have no actual impact on the environment. Labelling the United States as a country that is developing "still another generation of nuclear weapons" is supposed to illustrate Canada's moral superiority. But the fact that Canada has actually always been part of a nuclear armed alliance is forgotten. So too is the reality that the size of the U.S. nuclear arsenal has been reduced by two-thirds over the past decade.

Making every issue from Iraq, to Kyoto, to nuclear weapons, to the ICC a moral test of American foreign policy, and making the "Canadian way" the litmus test, has been a foolish way for Canada to conduct its international policy. This is particularly so when it is really a mixture of the ideology of national leaders and the search for domestic political gain that determines the content of Canadian international policy.

This approach to international policy has been irresponsible. It has squandered limited diplomatic capital and failed to advance the real interests of the Canadian people. It is an approach that Canada can no longer afford.

—NOTES—

[1] Tim Harper "PM's Private Jabs at Clinton Go Public Didn't Know Mike Was Live" *Toronto Star* (July 10, 1997) p. A1

[2] Ibid.

[3] Cited by Michael Hart "A New Accommodation with the United States: The Trade and Economic Dimension" *The Art of the State: Thinking North America* (IRPP Vol. 2 No. 2, 2005) p. 5

[4] Notes for an Address by the Honourable Pierre Pettigrew, Minister of Foreign Affairs, At the 2004 Scotiabank – AUCC Awards for Excellence in Internationalization, "Playing to Our Strength: Diversity and Canadian Foreign Policy" (Gatineau, Quebec, October 27, 2004)

[5] Notes for an Address by the Honourable Pierre Pettigrew, Minister of Foreign Affairs, At the 2004 Scotiabank – AUCC Awards for Excellence in Internationalization, "Playing to Our Strength: Diversity and Canadian Foreign Policy" (Gatineau, Quebec, October 27, 2004)

[6] Stuart Poore discusses this phenomenon in Stuart Poore, "Strategic Culture" in John Glenn, Darryl Howlett and Stuart Poore ed. *Neorealism vs. Strategic Culture* (Aldershot: Ashgate Publishing, 2004) p. 56

[7] Canada. Department of Foreign Affairs. *Canada in the World: Canadian Foreign Policy Review, 1995* Introduction.

[8] Canada. Department of National Defence. *Leadmark: The Navy's Strategy for 2020*, Part Six.

[9] Michael Ignatieff, "Peace Order and Good Government: A Foreign Policy Agenda for Canada" Skelton Lecture, Department of Foreign Affairs and International Trade, 12 March 2004

[10] Michael Adams, *Fire and Ice: The United States, Canada and the Myth of Converging Values* (Toronto: Penguin Canada, 2003) pp. 73–74

[11] Thomas S. Axworthy, "Unwilling to be Willing: The Primacy and Capability Principles in Canadian American Relations" (A Paper prepared for the Canadian Defence and Foreign Affairs Institute. May 2003) p. 18

[12] H. E. John Ralston Saul, "LaFontaine-Baldwin Symposium Inaugural Lecture" (Royal Ontario Museum, Toronto, March 23, 2000).

[13] Adams, *Fire and Ice,* p. 53

[14] Adams, *Fire and Ice,* p. 48.

[15] CTV News story "Canada-US Mutual Respect Declining: Poll" (May 9, 2005)

[16] Jack Jedwab, "Canadian Opinion on the Possible Invasion of Iraq—Between Old and New Europe" *Electronic Journal of the Association of Canadian Studies*, Table 4

[17] Dr. Pierre Martin and Dr. Michel Fortmann "Support for International Involvement in Canadian Public Opinion After the Cold War" *Canadian Military Journal* (Autumn 2001): 50

[18] Pew Research Center, "Americans Disengaging from Kosovo" (May 18, 1999)

[19] Centre for Research and Information on Canada, "Canadian and American Values: Distinct or Moving Toward Integration?" Canada & US – Support for War in Afghanistan (2002)

[20] Michael Hart "A New Accommodation with the United States: The Trade and Economic Dimension" *The Art of the State: Thinking North America* (IRPP Vol. 2 No. 2, 2005) pp. 6–7.

[21] See for instance David Frum's critique of Michael Adams' thesis in "David Frum's Diary" in *National Review Online* (November 9, 2003) [http://frum.nationalreview.com/archives/11092003.asp]; for Adams response see: Environics Press releases at: [http://erg.environics.net/news/default.asp?aID=548].

[22] Speech by Jack Granatstein to the conference of the Canadian Defence and Foreign Affairs Institute, Ottawa, October 31, 2005. Reported in Don Butler, "Pandering to Quebecers Hurts Nation" *National Post* (November 1, 2005) p. A6

[23] National Institute on Aging, National Stereotypes Common, Mistaken, Study Reports (October 6, 2005) [http://www.nia.nih.gov/NewsAndEvents/PressReleases/PR20051006.htm]

[24] William Renwick Riddell, *The Constitution of Canada in its History and Practical Working* (New Haven: Yale University Press, 1917) p. 149

[25] Prime Minister Mackenzie King quoted at the Imperial Conference, 1923 in: Michael Hart "A New Accommodation with the United States: The Trade and Economic Dimension" *The Art of the State: Thinking North America* (IRPP Vol. 2 No. 2, 2005) p. 3

[26] Hear clip of Truman's speech to the House of Commons, June 11, 1947 at: http://archives.cbc.ca/IDC-1-73-676-3866/politics_economy/presidents/clip2]

[27] James C. Bennett, *The Anglosphere Challenge: Why the English Speaking Nations will Lead the Way in the Twenty-First Century* (Rowan and Littlefield Publishers Inc. 2004)

[28] John Bryson "Trans-Atlantic Relations, the Bush Doctrine and the New World Order" (Directorate of Strategic Analysis, Department of National Defence, 2003) p. vii

[29] Gordon Smith "Establishing Canada's Priorities" in David Carment, Fen Osler Hampson and Norman Hillmer, *Canada Among Nations 2004: Setting Priorities Straight* (Montreal/Kingston: McGill-Aueen's University Press, 2005) p. 43 and p.45

[30] Lloyd Axworthy "Missile Counter-Attack" *Winnipeg Free Press* (March 3, 2005) p. A11

[31] US Embassy, "Address by U.S. Ambassador David H. Wilkins to a Combined Meeting of the Empire Club and Canadian Club of Toronto", November 14, 2005

[32] Alexander Panetta "Martin Out-Sources Search for National Identity to University Academic" Canadian Press Newswire (February 4, 2005)

[33] Lloyd Axworthy, "Canada and Human Security: the Need for Leadership" *International Journal* 52 (Spring 1997) p. 193

[34] Ibid. p. 192

[35] Canada. *Canada's International Policy Statement: A Role of Pride and Influence in the World* Overview Paper (2005) p. 22

[36] Michael Ignatieff, "Peace Order and Good Government: A Foreign Policy Agenda for Canada" Skelton Lecture, Department of Foreign Affairs and International Trade, 12 March 2004

[37] Jennifer Welsh, *At Home in the World: Canada's Global Vision for the 21st Century* (Toronto: Harper Collins, 2004) p. 189–190

[38] Canada25 *From Middle to Model Power: Recharging Canada's Role in the World.* Executive Summary

[39] Notes for an Address by the Honourable Lloyd Axworthy, Minister of Foreign Affairs on "Human Rights and Humanitarian Intervention" Washington DC, June 16, 2000

[40] Article VI, "Treaty on the Non-Proliferation of Nuclear Weapons" (signed July 1, 1968).

[41] Foreign Affairs Canada "The Comprehensive Nuclear Test Ban Treaty (CTBT) Introduction" [http://dfait-maeci.gc.ca/nndi-agency/ctbt_introduction-en.asp]

[42] Department of Foreign Affairs and International Trade, "Statement by Mr. Chris Westdal, Ambassador for Disarmament to the First Committee of the Fifty-Sixth Session of the General Assembly of the United Nations" (New York, October 10, 2001)

[43] Mines Action Canada, Anti-*Personnel Landmines: The Global Problem* [http://www.minesactioncanada.org/landmines/index.cfm?fuseaction=Start]

[44] Graeme Goldsworthy and Frank Faulkner "Armed Non-State Actors and the Ban on Anti-Personnel Mines" *The Journal of Humanitarian Assistance* (October 2003) [http://www.jha.ac/articles/a124.htm]

[45] Address by the Honourable Lloyd Axworthy to the Foreign Policy Association—"The Landmines Campaign in Context" (New York June 19, 1998)

[46] See Henry Kissinger, "The Pitfalls of Universal Jurisdiction: Risking Judicial Tyranny" *Foreign Affairs* (July/August 2001). At: [http://www.globalpolicy.org/intljustice/general/2001/07kiss.htm] While the Clinton administration signed the ICC treaty, it did so only to continue to be able to participate in future discussions related to the Court's mandate.

[47] Jeff Sallot "Cost of Kyoto Plan Pegged at $10 Billion" *Globe and Mail* (April 9, 2005) p. A6

[48] BBC News World Edition, "Kyoto Protocol Comes into Force" (February 16, 2005)

[49] CTVnews.ca "Dion: China Won't Agree to Emissions Targets" (September 3, 2005)

[50] Eileen Claussen, President of the Pew Center on Global Climate, quoted in the *Washington Post* February 16, 2005 p. A4.

[51] Canadian Manufacturers and Exporters, *Kyoto Alert* (no date) [http://www.cme-mec.ca/kyoto/documents/KyotoAlert.pdf]

[52] House of Commons. Hansard, Debates, October 9, 2002.

[53] Paul Heinbecker, "The UN in the Twenty-First Century" *Canada Among Nations* 2004 p. 255

CHAPTER 3

The Myth of Canada as a Global Power

O*ur destiny as a sovereign nation is inescapably tied to
our geography.*

–Allan Gotlieb, former Canadian ambassador to the United States

On a Sunday in November 1996, Prime Minister Jean Chrétien called his senior foreign affairs officials together for a crisis meeting. He had decided that Canada would lead a major military intervention in central Africa. The request for Canada to lead a mission to address an emerging humanitarian crisis in eastern Zaire came from the Clinton administration. The United States was facing considerable public pressure to do something about a growing crisis in which a million or more people were at risk from starvation and war. But in the aftermath of the Somalia debacle just three years earlier, there was considerable resistance within the administration to a lead American role. Instead, it was proposed that another country be found to take the point position.

It is most interesting that it was Canada that was approached to take on this role. Canada's military weaknesses were of course well known in Washington. Other countries were certainly more capable. But in Canada the Americans found a political leadership hungry for the media spotlight and unwilling to ask hard questions. Indeed, within one day the prime minister had already agreed. With Canada formally in the lead position, the United States was free to pull the strings behind the scenes and reduce or increase its support as it desired.

But Canada's ability to carry out the mission was dubious. Zaire was more than 12,000 kilometres away from Canada. The Canadian air force had no heavy-lift transport aircraft. Its 32 C-130 medium transport aircraft (of which perhaps three-quarters were "operationally available" at the time[1]) represented a modest airlift capacity. It had no overseas bases to support such a mission. It had no strategic or tactical reconnaissance capability to adequately assess the situation on the ground. It had no national intelligence agency, or indeed much of any expertise on the region and its conflict. The army had no rapid deployment capability since the airborne regiment had been disbanded a year previously. Neither did it have any heavy- or medium-lift helicopters, essential for operations in that part of the world.

As we now know, the mission became a fiasco. Nevertheless, in the House of Commons the prime minister described Canada's leadership of the mission as indicative of:

> ... a new world nation, without the burdens of history that weigh so many nations down ... a diverse bilingual country that knows the importance of accommodation and understanding ... [whose] only enemy is human suffering. Our only foe is hunger and disease. Our only adversary is pain and misery.[2]

Yet reality rudely intruded. Canada had neither the political clout nor the military muscle to mobilize the international support required to sustain the mission. As soon as the situation on the ground seemed to improve, American and other international support evaporated. Canada was left holding the bag. Hundreds of thousands of refugees may have been left in the jungle and the civil war in Zaire continued. It still rages to this day. Even so, the Canadian government declared "victory" and the troops were pulled out.

Within the Canadian military, the venture became known as the "bungle in the jungle."[3] Based on after-action reports, two foreign affairs and defence officials published a study that, among other things, concluded that:

> Canada did not have the influence to direct the [multi-national force] in ways its larger partners did not want to go, nor could Canada effectively influence the parties on the ground ... Canada had few levers beyond moral suasion to pressure larger nations ... Almost all troop-contributing nations, including Canada, made the presence of U.S. ground forces a condition of their participation ... By taking the lead without contributing combat troops, Canada was in a weak military and political position.[4]

Fast forward nearly a decade to another crisis in Africa, this time in the region of Darfur, Sudan. From the beginning of his administration, Paul Martin made Sudan a focal point of Canadian foreign policy in Africa. Between February 2004 and October 2005, government ministers and officials made at least 28 speeches and statements concerning the situation in Sudan. These called for a cessation of hostilities in the country and for "international action" to end the conflict. The latter was a call that the prime minister himself made at the United Nations in September 2004.[5]

The government took other steps to "look busy." It appointed a prime ministerial "personal representative" for Africa as well as a separate "special envoy for peace in Sudan." These individuals were tasked to attend meetings in both Canada (with concerned ethnic groups and NGOs) and overseas related to the crisis. In May 2005, the government announced that *up to* $170 million would be made available to support the "peace process" and the African Union Mission in Sudan (AMIS), which had the unenviable job of monitoring a region that is the size of France.

All the while, however, the war in Sudan has continued. Early in 2005, the death toll was estimated to be as high as several hundred thousand.[6] The United Nations in turn estimated that two million people had been made homeless.[7]

That Canada is trying to do something to provide humanitarian assistance in Sudan is, at face value, commendable. But motivations may not exactly be what they appear, and the means to act far too meager to support the rhetoric. In the case of Sudan, a partial motivation for providing increased assistance in 2005 may have been a political one: the need to secure the support of independent MP David Kilgour (a long-time advocate of a greater Canadian effort in Sudan) for the minority Liberal government in the House of Commons. The government came within one vote of being defeated in a spring non-confidence vote and one of Mr. Kilgour's conditions of continued support was a more active effort in Sudan.[8]

But the larger problem is that, contrary to government claims, Canada's limited regional profile, and light political and economic weight inevitably make it only a marginal player in that part of the world. Our trade with Sudan is negligible. In 2003, Canadian trade with Sudan was valued at just $42 million USD.[9] The only major Canadian economic presence in the country had been the controversial investments of Calgary-based Talisman Energy. But the company divested itself of these holdings in 2003. The relative unimportance of Sudan for the Canadian government was also evident in the fact that only one foreign affairs official was assigned to the Canadian embassy in Khartoum in 2004.[10] And while Canada is providing new humanitarian assistance as a result of the ongoing war, its historic aid levels to Sudan have been relatively low.[11]

Canada's limited economic and diplomatic weight has not been aided by our poor military capabilities. The combined weakness of all three undermines efforts to play an effective role in support of AMIS. AMIS's mandate is to monitor, observe and, where possible, assist the official peace process in Sudan—to the extent that one actually exists. Toward that end, the government authorized the deployment of up to about 60 Canadian military personnel to support AMIS. It wasn't much of an intervention force, so some equipment was also provided, most notably 100 old armoured personnel carriers, which were loaned to AMIS for one year. These were originally expected to be operational by mid-September 2005. Yet, initially, the Sudanese government simply refused to allow them into the country. It was not until mid-November that Canada was granted permission to ship them to Sudan from Senegal, where they had been stranded, and they were not expected to be fully operational before the end of 2005.[12]

In general terms, the dispersal of limited Canadian international resources and instruments usually makes Canada a supporting player on the world stage with little political clout. This is even the case with respect to countries much closer to us geographically—such as Haiti. While Canadian support is usually welcomed, its profile and influence is usually small because, in comparative terms, its overall "footprint" tends to be easily overshadowed by others. Afghanistan is a notable case in point.

Afghanistan is the largest recipient of Canadian international aid and also hosts the largest Canadian military presence abroad. However, Canada's $616 million in aid pledged over 8 years (from 2001 to 2009) constitutes about 4 percent of the $12.5 billion USD pledged by all international donors.[13] Similarly, while the Canadian military effort in Afghanistan has been in many ways exemplary, total troops deployed have usually averaged around 1,000 personnel—constituting perhaps 4 to 5 percent of total allied forces in the country.[14] While Canada did command the allied force policing Kabul for six months in 2004, and is taking a lead role in Kandahar from 2006, those roles, involving some 2,000 troops, constitute a maximum effort and are not sustainable indefinitely.

Quixotic statements suggesting that Canada can assume a major leadership role in rebuilding failed or failing states with which we have few historic connections, are partially grounded in a perception, at least by some politicians, that most Canadians won't know the difference. Still others actually believe their own rhetoric. They believe that influence in foreign policy is based more on what one says and how one says it, than on the capabilities that are actually brought to the table. In 1994, then-minister of foreign affairs André Ouellet commented that an independent foreign policy for Canada meant "first and foremost, hav[ing] the political courage to say what we think. To dare say what we think, sometimes in spite of others, to say it often before others, but also to always say it better than others."[15] This mentality seems to have grown stronger in recent years.

However, Canada is not a "global power" in as much as it is a "global dabbler." What Canadians need to understand is that if this country wants to have real influence on a particular problem in a way that actually furthers the national interest, then much greater focus in areas where we can actually make a difference will be required. The process of choosing where to focus must, in turn, be grounded on a clear understanding of just what the national interest in fact is.

Where Canada Ranks

In the years following World War II, when Canada was in a much stronger position within the international system, Canadian international policy focused largely on those parts of the world that mattered most to Canadian interests—North America, Europe, and East Asia. This focus permitted limited resources to be concentrated in a way that maximized the country's political influence. During the 1950s, Canada maintained a force of about 12,000 personnel in Europe: a 5,500-man brigade; an air division with 300 fighter aircraft; and it provided about $1 billion in mutual aid for the European allies. Simultaneously, Canada was able to deploy and sustain a full brigade for nearly three years of combat operations in Korea and lead a peacekeeping mission in Egypt in 1956. Canada's political influence in the alliance, and with key allies, was generally commensurate with this concentrated effort.[16]

Some have suggested that Canada's international role has grown naturally in the past decades; that it is now a "principal power" or "rule maker" in the international system. These suggestions first arose after Canada's admission to the G7 group of industrialized countries in 1975. This event encouraged some Canadian analysts to believe that, like France, Britain, Germany and Japan, Canada could be a major power in the international system.[17] However, this paradigm has largely ignored the real reason why Canada was admitted to the G7—an American desire to have another North American power at the table to provide support in economic discussions with Europe and Japan.[18] It also largely ignores the fact that since at least the mid-1960s Canada has never provided the resources necessary to play a major power role, and that none of the major powers really perceive Canada to be one of their equals, particularly in a military or political sense.

David Jones, formerly the political counsellor at the U.S. embassy, has pointedly summarized the perspective in Washington by stating: "Canada's lack of military weight renders it a peripheral player in international affairs and commensurately mutes its voice in any discussion about the security of North America."[19] According to former White House speech writer David Frum, international policy in Washington is generally made without considering Canada. "They just don't mention Canada", he says. "It would never occur to anybody that Canada would be able to contribute in an important way."[20] This is evidently also the perspective elsewhere. Indeed, only a few years ago, former French foreign minister Hubert Vedrine, ranked Canada below many other middle and regional powers in the international system.[21]

These perspectives are supported by the findings of a recent study conducted by the Canadian Institute of International Affairs (CIIA). The CIIA interviewed a cross section of 49 prominent international observers of Canadian international policy about their perspectives of Canada's "international impact." The study found that while "almost all interviewees expressed affection for Canada, the general view was that Canada's role has been marginal over the past 15 years." Indeed, American interviewees "observed that Canada has become almost irrelevant to U.S. foreign policy making." This, despite the fact that Canada spent some $243 billion on diplomacy, defence, and international development from 1989 to 2004.[22] This response suggests that neither the spending of money nor widely dispersed international activity necessarily translates into influence where it most matters. Larger geo-strategic realities are involved that make both policy focus and effective coordination a prerequisite for real effectiveness.

Canada and "Globalization"

It is ironic that from the 1960s onward, as Canada progressively lost influence internationally, its declaratory policy became bolder and its efforts became more dispersed and global in scope. This global scope to Canada's international policy has become particularly pronounced over the past decade.

While this policy orientation partly flows from the idea that Canadian values must be shared with the world, in recent years the policy has also been justified by the perceived impact of "globalization" on Canada. A policy paper produced by the Privy Council Office (PCO) in 2003 defined globalization as: "the increasing integration of economies and societies." It is argued that globalization:

> is reaching new heights, fuelled by exponential increases in trade and financial flows and the information revolution. ... Governments around the world are grappling with ways to navigate through an increasingly complex policy arena .... [it has] intensified and deepened interdependencies among nations and among issues. [23]

The PCO paper asserts that, "Based on the standard measures of information technology, finance, trade, travel, personal communications and international engagement, Canada is in fact considered to be one of the most globalized nations in the world."[24] The International Policy Statement (IPS) of 2005 argues that the global economy is changing "in two fundamental ways":

> First, ideas have become the engine of productivity and the currency of global success. ... Second, today's business models are driven not by geography, but by investment decisions and information technology. Companies are moving toward global supply chains. As international commerce increasingly shifts production, design and other business activities around the world, Canada faces new competition for markets, skilled workers, leading edge technology and foreign direct investment.[25]

This may be true in a macroeconomic sense. However, even though modern business models may increasingly be driven by factors "other than geography", Canadian economic interests nevertheless remain, remarkably, geographically focused. In 1972, British strategist Colin Gray wrote that: "Canadian politicians cannot escape from a number of geographical facts." He argued that these encompassed several overarching realities, including the facts that:

> Canada and the United States, share the North American continent; secondly, that the United States is the only foreign country sharing a land frontier with Canada; thirdly, that Canada, in important respects, lies "between" the United States and its major potential adversaries; fourthly that encompasses the second largest land area in the world; and finally, that Canada enjoys the longest coastline in the world.

Gray argued that "physical geography will offer resistance to policy, regardless of will-power in Ottawa."[26] Geography is the most important factor in determining Canada's general international rank and status. In many respects, Canada may be large in absolute terms, but it is small, particularly in an economic and military sense, given its geographic context.

Measured in economic terms, there has been a trend toward greater integration in North America. In the past several decades, the percentage of Canadian trade with the United States has grown from 64 percent in 1975, to 69 percent in 1983, to 75 percent in 2005. A staggering 87 percent of Canadian exports are destined for the United States.[27] As Table 3 illustrates, Canada is one of only a few countries that is almost totally dependent on a single large trading partner.

When one compares Canada's trade with the United States with the level of trade conducted by other states with their number one trading partners, the degree of Canadian dependence on the United States is readily apparent. Even small states, such as Denmark, Ireland, New Zealand, and the Czech Republic, which, in relative terms, are situated next to comparative economic giants, do not have the degree of trade dependency on that larger trading partner that Canada has on the United States. Only Mexico, also caught in the American orbit, has a similar level of trade dependency.

The economic relationship between Canada and the United States is often described as one of mutual interdependence. Indeed, just under 20 percent of total U.S. trade is conducted with Canada. However, this cross border trade of goods and services with Canada actually only translates into about 4 percent of America's total GDP (vs. 53 percent for Canada).

The United States' huge internal market effectively makes the relationship asymmetrical.[28] While Canada's economic importance is obviously magnified in the northern border states, its overall economic profile in the U.S. is actually fairly small in relative terms.

Table 3: Comparative Dependency on a Single Trading Partner, Combined Imports and Exports—Canada and Selected Countries, 2003

Country	Top Trading Partner	Percent of Total Trade with That State
Germany	France	10
United Kingdom	United States	13
Norway	Germany	13
Australia	Japan	15
France	Germany	17
United States	Canada	20
Denmark	Germany	21
New Zealand	Australia	22
Ireland	United Kingdom	24
Israel	United States	26
Czech Republic	Germany	35
Mexico	United States	74
Canada	**United States**	**75**

Source: International Monetary Fund, *Direction of Trade Statistics Yearbook, 2004*

While economic relations with the rest of the world remain important (totalling $122.6 billion USD in two-way trade in 2003[29]), particularly for certain sectors of the economy, global trade will always be overshadowed by Canada's trading relations with the United States.

The IPS asserts that "emerging giants" such as China, India, and Brazil are "making their presence felt" in the global economy. This is true, but for the most part their relative presence in the Canadian economy remains small. Even if Canadian trade with such states were to expand somewhat disproportionately over the next several years, that presence would still remain quite small. Many of these states are largely a source of cheap consumer goods. Indeed, in the case of China—now Canada's second most important trading partner—Canada imports four times as much from that country as it sells to it (over $12 billion USD in imports vs. just over $3 billion USD in exports in 2003). [30]

That Canada trades with the rest of the world does not mean that it must, or can, conduct a complementary global foreign policy with equal vigour in all parts of the world. Not only is this not feasible, it is simply not a national imperative. In this respect Derek Burney argues that: "Our objectives in trade policy need to reflect genuine Canadian aspirations and not be manufactured like instant meals, to provide a convenient press release for sudden prime ministerial or ministerial visit."[31]

As Table 4 illustrates, Canada's footprint in the economies of other countries is almost always relatively small, the United States being the only major exception. Because of the opportunities afforded Canada by the American market, increased trade with the U.S. has completely eclipsed the growth of trade with the rest of the world. This is partly why the policy of trade diversification, as pursued in the 1970s, failed. Despite government policy of that period, the percentage of Canadian trade with the rest of the world actually declined rather than increased, and the percentage of trade conducted with the United States continued to grow.[32]

Table 4: Percentage of Trade, Imports and Exports, with Canada's Top Seven Trading Partners plus Brazil and India, 2003

Country	Percentage of Canadian Trade with That State	Percentage of That State's Trade with Canada
India	0.29	1
Brazil	0.39	1.4
France	1	0.65
Germany	1.5	0.6
Mexico	1.9	2.1
United Kingdom	2	1.7
Japan	3	1.7
China	3.1	1.2
United States	75	20

Source: International Monetary Fund, Direction of Trade Statistics Year Book, 2004

It is readily apparent that today neither any single state nor even any conceivable combination of states, provides a realistic alternative to the continued centrality of the Canada-U.S. economic relationship.

Canada is a North American Power, not a Global One

The authors of the 2003 study *In the National Interest* were quite correct to assert that the United States "is the only real imperative" in Canadian foreign policy.[33] As a North American state, Canada's fate, its continued prosperity and its security will always remain tied to that of the United States; a fact that has led Allan Gotlieb to conclude, correctly, that "our destiny as a sovereign nation is inescapably tied to our geography."[34] If one looks at the facts of Canada's economic relationship with the United States, this is indeed the case. Canada is really less a global economic power today than it is a North American economic power. That will not change. Indeed, the IPS itself acknowledges that Canada actually needs "a more expansive partnership" with the United States "to reflect the unique circumstances of our continent".[35]

With respect to defence and security matters, how "global" are Canada's interests? Some, such as former Minister of National Defence Bill Graham, have argued that: "In a globalized world, our own security is inextricably linked to the security of those beyond our borders."[36] Owing to the values focus of international policy, there have been few, if any, limitations on this concept. In the 1994 Defence White Paper, security threats and challenges were broadly defined to include refugees, failed states, the "resurgence of old hatreds", weapons proliferation, and generally "global pressures."[37] In keeping with this policy orientation, the Canadian Forces were deployed on missions on nearly every continent in a ten-year period. Similarly, Canada's development assistance and diplomacy have had no particular geographic focus.

The IPS of 2005 continued this orientation asserting that:

> The Government also recognizes the importance of meeting threats to our security as far away from our borders as possible, wherever they may arise. Security in Canada ultimately begins with stability abroad.[38]

While in a very general sense "stability abroad" may be in the country's interest, Canada cannot contribute equally and effectively to stability everywhere. Our performance in Zaire and Sudan dramatically illustrates this. Such a policy prescription, difficult even for a super power, is infeasible for a small to middle-sized power. It also makes it more difficult to set policy priorities focused on countering the most direct security threats.

Both the National Security Policy of 2004 and the IPS argued that Canada would attempt to fill such a niche by assisting "failed and failing states." However, as Professors David Bercuson and Denis Stairs noted "the global agenda is massive."[39] The IPS noted that decisions on where to engage would be made on a "case-by-case" basis based on the country's interests and values.[40] This provided little direction as to exactly how the Canadian government would decide where to engage and where not to engage. Certainly Queen's University Professor Kim Richard Nossal is partly correct in his assertion that "Canadians can rest easy – the extravagant ideals articulated in the International Policy Statement are in fact not to be taken seriously ... these ideals are nothing more than feel-good and sound-good rhetoric."[41] Unfortunately, however, rhetoric often has a life of its own and results in demands for a semblance of action. This means that any agenda based in the general goals of the IPS would be based less on the national interest or on real linkages that may exist between Canada and a given country, than on the media profile of a particular issue and on resource drivers.

But in the absence of a high degree of political, social, cultural, strategic, and economic expertise specific to particular societies and cultures, a strategy of rebuilding shattered communities and societies is unlikely to be successful. Neither are we likely to sustain the prolonged commitment of immeasurable resources that are required.

Moreover, since our foreign policy is global, we usually don't know where we are going until a crisis actually erupts. This makes the accumulation of real expertise on a particular country or region nearly impossible. And once we commit ourselves to one particular mission, our global pretensions soon lead to new demands to take on a yet another role somewhere else. This is hardly the recipe for a successful policy and it leaves Canada little real ability to play a significant, let alone a decisive, role.

The development agenda outlined in the IPS faces similar problems. Although there is a nominal intent to focus a portion of Canada's bilateral development assistance on 25 specific countries, this agenda continues to cast the net widely by including countries and societies on different continents that are very different. Canada's real policy expertise and ability to help is inevitably limited in such an approach.

Despite the inherent difficulties in pursuing a truly global international policy, the orientation has not been seriously questioned. Rob McRae, the director of policy planning in the Department of Foreign Affairs recently wrote that: "The question as to whether Canada should pursue a global or a regional international policy, much loved by the pundits, has not really taken off at the political level."[42]

There seem to be several reasons for this. The first reason is a product of inertia and bureaucratic interests. For the past 30 years, Canadian international policy has progressively become more global in scope, in part driven by the bureaucratic interests of the Department of Foreign Affairs. Within the Department, one of the strongest perceptions is that there is no area of the world from which Canada can afford to withdraw or even seriously lessen its engagement.

The second reason is grounded once again in the desire of Canadian politicians to score points with ethnic communities in the country. In the last several decades, the country's population has become increasingly diverse. Ten percent of Canadians have origins in the Asia-Pacific region, 20 percent of recent immigrants come from the Middle East and North Africa, and 4 percent come from sub-Saharan Africa.[43] However, the idea that Canadian foreign policy should express the ethnic origins of every Canadian makes it nearly impossible to make that policy effective. It disperses international policy efforts over scores of countries, most of which simply have no relevance to Canada in an economic, political, or strategic sense. Our diplomatic involvement with most of these states is devoid of political weight, largely symbolic and, more often than not, totally irrelevant.

The fact that one million Canadians are of Chinese origin and 700,000 are of Indian origin does not necessarily translate into enhanced security and economic interests for Canada as a whole. About three and one-half million Canadians are of German origin, yet Canada's trade with Germany amounts to only 1.5 percent of its total world trade. Similarly, there are about eight million francophones in Canada, yet only one percent of its world trade is with France.

Neither is there much evidence to support the view that ethnic links significantly contribute to enhanced influence in a particular country or region. Canada's limited influence in India and Pakistan was exposed in 1998 when Canada sharply curtailed relations with both countries to "punish" them for their nuclear tests. However, the problem was neither country seemed to notice. Canada's economic and strategic presence in that part of the world is simply too small to make an impact. After a few years, Ottawa had to retreat from that policy approach even though there had been absolutely no change in either country's nuclear policy.

The third reason is that in a values-driven international policy, it becomes extremely difficult to make hard choices based on interests. Values, which of course allow for no compromises, are potentially engaged everywhere and for the ideologically motivated, the question of potential disengagement, even if such disengagement is based on geopolitical realities, becomes extremely difficult to face. Everything becomes a priority, which means that, in reality, there are no priorities.

The result is an international policy that is ever more dispersed and increasingly less relevant to advancing real economic and strategic interests. That will only change if both hard choices are made and real focus on real priorities is restored to our international policy.

—NOTES—

[1] Based on a publicly stated availability rate of C-130s at the time of the Kosovo conflict. National Defence press briefing, April 4, 1999.

[2] Canada. House of Commons, Debates, 35th Parliament, 3rd Session, Vol. 5 (November 18, 1996) pp. 6380–81

[3] See: Roy Rempel, *The Chatter Box: An Insider's Account of the Irrelevance of Parliament in the Making of Canadian Foreign and Defence Policy* (Toronto: Breakout Educational Network/Dundurn Press, 2002) pp. 163–172.

[4] James Appathurai and Ralph Lysyshyn, "Lessons Learned from the Zaire Mission" *Canadian Foreign Policy* 5, No. 2 (Winter 1998) pp. 93–105

[5] See: [http://dfait-maeci.gc.ca/Africa/sudan-crisis-in-darfur-en.asp]

[6] For an indictment of the western response to the Sudanese atrocities see: Christopher Hitchens "Realism in Darfur" (November 7, 2005) [www.slate.com/id/212967/]

[7] BBC "How Many Have Died in Darfur" (February 16, 2005) [BBC: http://news.bbc.co.uk/1/hi/world/africa/4268733.stm]

[8] Canadian Press "Canada to Send 150 Troops to Sudan Missions" (May 8, 2005); For the Government's denial of this charge: CTV News Story "Graham Denies Sudan Aid is to Secure MPs Vote" (May 9, 2005)

[9] International Monetary Fund, *Direction of Trade Statistics Yearbook, 2004* p. 119

[10] Source: Department of Foreign Affairs, Access to Information Request A-2004–00285. By 2005, the number of Canadians assigned to the Khartoum mission had increased to four persons.

[11] This aid totalled about $14 million in 2000–01, $10 million in 2001–02 and $11 million in 2002–03. CIDA, *Statistical Report on Development Assistance, Fiscal Year 2002-03*, (CIDA, Statistical Analysis Section, March 2004) p. 29

[12] Report on CBC Newsworld, November 15, 2005.

[13] This amount was pledged at the Berlin conference on Afghanistan's reconstruction in March 2004.

[14] Figure based on a total of about 17,000 American and 8,000 allied (c. 1,200 of which are Canadian) troops in Afghanistan in 2004–05.

[15] Department of Foreign Affairs André Ouellet, "Address to the Parliamentary Debate on Canada's Foreign Policy Review" *Statements and Speeches*, 94/11 (March 15, 1994) p. 1

[16] For a discussion see: Roy Rempel, *Counterweights: The Failure of Canada's German and European Policy, 1955-1995* (Montreal/Kingston: McGill-Queen's University Press, 1996) pp. 110–132

[17] The principal book in this regard was: David Dewitt and John Kirton, *Canada as a Principal Power: A Study in Foreign Policy and International Relations* (Toronto: John Wiley, 1983)

[18] West Germany was also prepared to support Canada's admission as a quid pro quo for Canada maintaining its small, but symbolically important, military presence in Europe. For discussion see: Roy Rempel and Wilhelm Bleek, "Defence and Economic Linkages in Canadian-German Relations: 1969–1982" *Canadian Foreign Policy* 7 (Spring 2000): 81–98.

[19] David Jones, "Canada-U.S. Relations After September 11: Back to Basics" *Policy Options* (March 2002): 26

[20] underground royal commission interview with David Frum, March 27, 2004.

[21] Vedrine asserted that Canada could only be considered part of a middle-ranking group of countries by virtue of its membership in organizations like

the G8 and NATO. Hubert Vedrine, dialogue with Dominique Moisi, *Les cartes de la France a l'heure de la mondialisation* (Paris: Librarie Artheme Fayard, 2000) pp. 14–15

[22] Robert Greenhill, *Making a Difference? External Views on Canada's International Impact* (Canadian Institute of International Affairs, February 2005) pp. 3, 4, and 10.

[23] Privy Council Office. Report of the International Policy Framework Task Force, *Toward an International Policy Framework for the 21st Century* (July 2003) p. 1 and p. 2

[24] Privy Council Office. *Toward an International Policy Framework for the 21st Century* (July 2003) p. 14

[25] *Canada's International Policy Statement: A Role of Pride and Influence in the World* Overview Paper (2005) p. 2

[26] Colin Gray, *Canadian Defence Priorities: A Question of Relevance* (Toronto: Clarke, Irwin and Company, 1972) p. 15

[27] International Monetary Fund, *Direction of Trade Statistics Yearbooks, 1982, 1985 and 2004.*

[28] William Robson, *The North American Imperative: A Public Good Framework for Canada-U.S. Economic and Security Cooperation*, (C.D. Howe Commentary, Border Papers Series, October 2004) pp. 13–14

[29] International Monetary Fund, *Direction of Trade Statistics Yearbook, 2004*

[30] International Monetary Fund, *Direction of Trade Statistics Yearbook 2004* p. 120

[31] Derek H. Burney, "Foreign Policy: More Coherence, Less Pretence" (Simon Riesman Lecture in International Trade Policy, Carleton University, March 14, 2005) p. 17

[32] The policy of trade diversification also failed because of the uncoordinated way in which the Trudeau government implemented it. See: Roy Rempel, *Counterweights: The Failure of Canada's German and European Policy, 1955-1995* (Montreal/Kingston: McGill-Queen's University Press, 1996)

[33] Canadian Defence and Foreign Affairs Institute, *In the National Interest: Canadian Foreign Policy in an Insecure World*, (October, 2003) p. viii.

[34] Allan Gotlieb, "Romanticism and Realism in Canada's Foreign Policy" (Toronto: C.D. Howe Institute, Benefactors Lecture, November 3, 2004) p. 39

[35] *Canada's International Policy Statement: A Role of Pride and Influence in the World* Overview Paper (2005) p. 6

[36] Notes for an Address by the Honourable Bill Graham, Minister of Foreign Affairs, on the Occasion of the Launch of Canada's First United Nations Humanitarian Appeal, Ottawa Ontario November 19, 2003

[37] Canada. Department of National Defence, *1994 Defence White Paper* pp. 4–6

[38] *Canada's International Policy Statement: A Role of Pride and Influence in the World* Defence Paper (2005) p. 2

[39] David J. Bercuson and Denis Stairs "Canada's International Policy Statement: What's New, What's Old, And What is Needed" *In the Canadian Interest? Assessing Canada's International Policy Statement* (Canadian Defence and Foreign Affairs Institute, November 2005) p. 4

[40] *Canada's International Policy Statement: A Role of Pride and Influence in the World* Diplomacy Paper (2005) p. 22

[41] Kim Richard Nossal. "The Responsibility to be Honest" *In the Canadian Interest? Assessing Canada's International Policy Statement* p. 42

[42] Rob McRae "International Policy Reviews in Perspective" in David Carment, Fen Osler Hampson and Norman Hillmer ed. *Canada Among Nations 2004* (Montreal: McGill-Queen's, 2005) p.63

[43] *Canada's International Policy Statement: A Role of Pride and Influence in the World*, Diplomacy Paper pp. 24–27

CHAPTER 4

Multilateralism and Morality in International Policy

The limits of UN declarations are not the limits of Canadian foreign policy or our security needs.

–Stephen Harper, prime minister (then leader of the Opposition)

On March 20, 2003, 150,000 American, British, and Australian troops crashed across the Iraqi border and invaded Saddam Hussein's Iraq. The impact of American actions in Iraq, for good or ill, will be debated by historians for years to come, but the decision taken was the product of the fundamental change in American strategic thinking that occurred as a result of 9/11. In the final analysis, the American decision to invade corresponded with the actions taken by great powers throughout history in defence of their vital interests. It was a reminder that even in the modern world, in the words of the Prussian strategist Karl von Clausewitz, war remains a tool for "the continuation of policy by other means."

In the weeks prior to the war, the reaction of many in Canada's foreign policy elite to the American military build-up was one of visceral outrage and anger. They deplored the unilateral nature of the action and the fact that the United Nations Security Council had been bypassed. For some, the very idea of using force to remove Saddam Hussein from power was something that should be opposed regardless of whether it was sanctioned by the Security Council or not. From both within the government and without, they strongly pressed the government to oppose any military action. In the end, their view won out. In a very public way, Canada came out in strong opposition. Indeed, on April 8, Prime Minister Chrétien told the House of Commons that:

> Canada took a principled stand against participating in military intervention in Iraq. ... We argued that a multilateral approach through the United Nations was key to enhancing the interna-

tional legitimacy of military action and would make it easier
after the war was over. We applied these principles in deciding not
to join the coalition when the war began without a new resolution
of the Security Council. The decision on whether or not to send
troops into battle must always be a decision of principle. Not a decision of economics. Not even a decision of friendship alone.[1]

Many Canadians might believe that the government took a principled
and wise decision not to participate. In reality, however, neither principle
nor wisdom had much to do with it.

It is difficult to know whether the prime minister really believed what
he said on April 8. Perhaps, on a superficial level, he did. However, the
inconsistencies in Canadian policy suggested otherwise. For one, if
Canada objected to the war "on principle", why then were serving
Canadian soldiers participating in the invasion? Canadian soldiers, seconded to allied units, have served in Iraq since the start of the war. In
2003–04, Canadian Major-General Walt Natynczyk even served as a
deputy commander of U.S. forces in Baghdad.[2] Since any Canadian military contribution is inevitably largely symbolic, the tasking of a two-star
general to serve as part of the U.S. command staff in Baghdad does not
support the notion that Canada opposed the war "on principle."

The notion that Canada always insists on UN approval for military
action is also inaccurate. Just five years previously, in 1998, the Chrétien
government had formally supported American and British air strikes
against Iraq without any specific UN authorization. Then, in 1999, it
tasked Canadian CF-18 fighters to participate in NATO's war in Kosovo
even though, again, there was no Security Council mandate to do so. In
fact, initially Canada had been moving in the same direction on Iraq as
the United States. In February 2003, Canada deployed one its command
and control destroyers to the Persian Gulf to assume command of *Task
Force 151*—a joint allied naval command. The Americans permitted
Canada to lead this force on the informal understanding that Canada
would openly support the coming military campaign in Iraq.[3] If this was
their understanding, they were soon going to be disappointed.

The issue of Iraq is a difficult and controversial one. In light of what
has happened in Iraq and the fact that the United States and its allies have
become bogged down in a prolonged counter insurgency campaign, many
Canadians would probably conclude that Canada made the right deci-

sion to limit its involvement. However, if the right decision was made from a Canadian interest perspective, then it was done so inadvertently. What the Canadian government has done with regard to Iraq is to involve itself militarily, in largely a covert fashion, but to publicly try to take the moral high ground in opposition to the war. This hypocrisy undermines Canada's credibility in Washington and is contrary to the national interest.

Prime Minister Chrétien claimed that "a multilateral approach" was the key principle underscoring Canada's approach to the conflict in Iraq. When the United States decided to move ahead without Security Council authorization, Chrétien said that Canada simply could not participate. However, the evidence suggests that Canada's commitment to this principle is intermittent and is upheld as much in the breach as in the observance. It is also evident that domestic political considerations, in the case of Iraq, the perceived interests of the Liberal Party in the then pending Quebec provincial elections, are often at least as important as principle and the commitment to multilateralism.

Despite these inconsistencies, the idea that multilateralism must be Canada's primary source of moral authority in international affairs is common within Canada's international policy establishment. Indeed, some argue that it is the *raison d'etre* of Canadian international policy.

The argument in this chapter is that this idea is not only false, but it also effectively sidelines the interests of the Canadian people. It overshadows, and even supplants, the primary responsibility that any democratically elected government has to its citizens, with an allegiance to international organizations whose interests and objectives may actually stand in opposition to Canadian interests. In this sense, the idea that multilateralism is the primary source of moral authority for Canada's international policy should be discarded.

What Multilateralism Is and Is Not

Multilateralism has been a consistent theme in Canadian foreign policy since, at least, our key role in founding both the UN and NATO in the 1940s. But its accompanying ambitions have grown progressively larger and at the same time less realistic. By 2005, the IPS described effective multilateralism as an "essential tool in preserving the Canadian approach" to international policy and offered three principal rationales.[4]

First, multilateralism is said to serve Canadian interests. But in what sense? There is little question that there are certain unique advantages that accrue to a country like Canada from multilateral diplomacy. Skillful diplomacy enables small powers to build coalitions that facilitate the establishment principles, norms, and rules that are to their advantage. Canadian engagement in the World Trade Organization, for instance, can help to build global trade rules that can provide crucial support for Canadian trade objectives. Similarly, Canadian engagement in a process such as the Law of the Sea can help draft international laws, rules, and regulations that correspond with the country's maritime interests.

However, as illustrated in chapter two, the concurrence of the major powers, particularly the United States, is almost always central for establishing new and effective international legal regimes. Sustained and quiet diplomacy is the best tool to achieve such objectives. Such diplomacy seldom achieves dramatic overnight success. It may rarely be the kind of diplomacy that attracts much media attention. But when such regimes are effectively established, they are usually the most effective means for advancing Canada's political interests.

Second, multilateralism is said to facilitate the resolution of global problems. While it is not a panacea for success in every case, it is certainly true that multilateralism often allows resources to be pooled in order to address global challenges and concerns. This is the case whether one is confronted with a particular security problem or trying to marshal an international response to a major regional disaster.

A third rationale is the most dubious: namely that multilateralism can act as a counterweight to American influence. This rationale flows from the notion that American values, in important respects, are different from Canadian ones. In this regard, the IPS stated that: "Without such [multilateral] forums, and without a strong Canadian presence in them, we risk subjecting ourselves to the wishes of those who may not act in accordance with our priorities."[5] In a speech the day before the IPS was released, Prime Minister Martin seemed to clarify what this statement meant when he said that Canada would not "become a 'handmaiden' to any superpower."[6]

This perspective runs deep in Canadian foreign policy. It is acknowledged in a Privy Council Task Force report of 2003, which asserts that: "While Canada clearly has much to gain from its close economic ties with the world's largest economy, in the post 9/11 North America—where security trumps trade—it also has much to lose." The paper goes on to argue that if Canada fails to find counterweights to the United States globally, it will reduce Ottawa's ability to:

- shape global rules and institutions
- protect and promote substantial economic and security benefits derived from our relationship with the U.S.
- protect Canadians from global threats of terrorism, disease, and crime
- safeguard sovereignty by ceding leadership to others.[7]

On the surface, these concerns appear to be legitimate. But it is far from certain that in a unipolar world (a world with only one superpower) global engagement and *activity* in international organizations can realistically and practically counterbalance a power like the United States. When a major power has no strategic rivals, then allies and support from international organizations may well be less important than they are in a bipolar world. There may therefore be few practical opportunities or relevant international forums in which to counterbalance the United States.[8]

A more fundamental question on most issues is, why would we want to? In our relationship with the rest of the world, Canadian and American strategic and economic interests are almost always closely analogous. While there will be discrete issues on which the two countries will have differing interests, as a general principle the strategic unity of North America does not make counterbalancing the United States a sound basis for Canadian foreign policy in a unipolar world. It is certainly never a rational policy approach when the issue over which we might disagree is peripheral to Canada's hard interests.

Even so, many Canadian politicians continue to believe in the unlimited potential of this brand of multilateralism. But Canadian diplomacy at the UN in the lead-up to the Iraq war had no impact in constraining the United States from military action in that crisis. Neither is there any evidence that global engagement or activity does anything to enhance Canadian sovereignty in the context of a North American relationship in which Canada and the United States are increasingly integrated.

While the first two rationales see multilateralism as a tool of policy, this third perspective has come to view multilateralism as a kind of end in itself; as a means to enhance Canada's independence from the United States. In part, this flows from Canada's political tradition. Canadian political scientist William Hogg points to a "functionalist" fixation in Canadian foreign policy—meaning the integration of Canada in multilateral frameworks at every possible opportunity—a fixation he describes as almost "pathological".[9]

One element of this perspective is the belief that engagement in international organizations carries important moral authority. This approach to multilateral engagement partially explains why Canada has come to be described as the world's "great joiner" state. There are few international organizations of which Canada is not a part and, although IPS asserted that in future the Government would put "outcome ahead of process", there was no likelihood that the Martin government would de-emphasize the importance of any organization of which Canada is a member.

Much of Canada's multilateralism is in fact almost exclusively process driven. A Privy Council Office policy paper attempts to illustrate how important multilateralism is for Canada by noting that between 1989 and 1999 the country signed about 235 multilateral and 374 bilateral treaties and agreements.[10] However, the substantive value of many of these agreements is unknown. Since nearly every international process has a political requirement to produce some sort of agreement, communiqué, or memorandum of understanding, the relevance of such statistics is questionable.

In the end, much of Canada's commitment to multilateralism is ideological in nature. There are few places where this is more evident than in the country's United Nations policy. As Douglas Bland has noted, many Canadians regard the UN as the moral "legitimizer" for all international actions in which the country is involved.[11] This belief is, however, simply false.

The UN Cannot Work as We Believe It Should

Canada's commitment to the United Nations is rooted in the three rationales for multilateralism already discussed—interests, ensuring effectiveness, and maintaining a counterweight to the United States. In the context of the *de facto* elevation of multilateralism as an end in itself, the United Nations has come to be viewed as an indispensable institution in Canadian foreign policy. In this sense, it is perceived to stand at the moral centre of Canadian international policy. In large measure this is because the UN is seen to be as "at the heart of the development of international law."[12]

This perspective is evident in many official government statements. The 1995 Foreign Policy White Paper argued that:

> The UN continues to be the key vehicle for pursuing Canada's global security objectives. Canada can best move forward its global security priorities by working with other member states. The success of the UN is fundamental, therefore, to Canada's future security.[13]

This remains the orientation of policy a full decade later. The "renewal of the multilateral system" with the UN at its heart is a core objective of the IPS.[14] Prime Minister Martin laid the groundwork for this orientation in a speech delivered in January 2004, in which he stated that if the UN doesn't work,

> then let's not kid ourselves, the work of every national capital will be severely hobbled. The United Nations has to work because it reminds us, like no other institution that all nations have interests that demand recognition, and that all nations have responsibilities towards each other that they cannot shirk. The UN stands at the centre of the global vision—battered but crucial to defend—that says: it either works for all, or it doesn't work at all.[15]

There is little question that on many issues the United Nations can serve Canadian interests. However, the idea that "the UN is fundamental to Canada's future security" or that the UN must "either work for all or it doesn't work at all", is illustrative of ideology running away with reality. Essentially, there are two principal reasons why the UN cannot function as currently envisaged by many Canadians.

The Question of Effectiveness

As an international security organization the UN is both chronically ineffective and cannot be substantively reformed. This ineffectiveness is inherent in the nature of the international system. The UN was originally envisaged as an institution that would be able to maintain international peace and security through the collective action of member states. But for the United Nations to function as envisaged, all states must be prepared to subordinate their interests to the ideals of collective security. In this respect, General (now Senator) Romeo Dallaire urges that:

> the only solution ... is a revitalized and reformed international institution charged with maintaining the world's peace and security, supported by the international community and guided by the founding principles of its Charter and the Universal Declaration of Human Rights. The UN must undergo a renaissance if it is to be involved in conflict resolution. ... [This] must encompass the member nations, who need to rethink their roles and recommit to a renewal of purpose.[16]

Yet states simply do not perceive and interpret the founding principles of the UN Charter or their obligations under the Universal Declaration of Human Rights in the same way. Nor do they subordinate their national interests to the concept of collective security as ideally defined by Western liberals.

It has always been the case that once states are confronted with the reality of a crisis in a particular region of the world, they usually assess their level of involvement and action in terms of their interests. While states are sometimes prepared to act in a given crisis solely on the basis of humanitarian considerations, hard economic, political, and strategic interests are usually required to sustain that involvement. Nor is it realistic to expect that such temporary and emergency interventions will likely solve political and social problems with very deep roots. Experiences in Haiti, the Congo, and other places over the past decade bear this out. Democratically elected governments, in particular, will find it difficult to justify the expense of blood and treasure to sustain a commitment if the national interest in a particular region or country is seen to be weak.

The larger and more geographically (or otherwise) diverse the membership of an international organization, the greater the difficulty it is to formulate a decision-making consensus on contentious questions. And the UN today is composed of 191 member states with leaders as different as Kim Jong-il, George Bush, Robert Mugabe, Vladimir Putin, the Chinese communist party leadership, the Iranian mullahs, and so on.

There are only two occasions in history where the United Nations has been able to act in keeping with its principal mandate—that of ensuring global and regional collective security. The first occurred in 1950, when the UN Security Council approved and supported American intervention to defend South Korea against communist aggression, while the second happened in 1990–91 when the Security Council sanctioned an American-led campaign to expel Iraqi forces from Kuwait.

Yet, even these two events were anomalies. UN action in 1950 was possible only because the Soviet Union happened to be boycotting the Security Council at the time (something that it never did again) and because Taiwan was still sitting on the Security Council in the seat representing China. In 1990–91, the Security Council decision to sanction the American campaign against Iraq partly flowed from the weakness of the then dying Soviet Union and partly from the fact that no other state (great power or otherwise; Arab or non-Arab) was willing to risk confrontation with the United States for the sake of Saddam Hussein.

On all other occasions in which states have resorted to war since 1945, those actions have not been sanctioned by the Security Council in advance. On both occasions (Korea and Kuwait) where the Security Council specifically authorized the use of force, it was done to support military action that the United States would have undertaken in any case. Even in these two cases, the UN's involvement was a sideshow.

This means that the United Nations has been shown to be as irrelevant on international security questions as was the League of Nations in the interwar period (1919 to 1939). The League became increasingly ineffective in the period between the two world wars because the major powers could not be convinced to intervene decisively in matters where their national interests were not seen as vitally engaged. With the benefit of hindsight this may have a mistake for those countries (and indeed the world), but it was inevitable in the absence of an ability to foretell the future. In the League Council, the unanimous consent of all member states was required to take any decision. Hence deadlock prevented any effective steps from being taken to prevent the Japanese occupation of Manchuria in 1931 or the Italian invasion of Ethiopia in 1935.

While the United Nations Security Council only requires the agreement of 9 of 15 member states to take action in a crisis, any of the 5 permanent members can also veto a given decision. Even though this approval threshold is less than that which was required in the League of Nations, it has often proven to be an insurmountable barrier for taking action in particular crises (notably in Rwanda or in Kosovo). In other crises (such as Croatia, Bosnia or, more recently, Sudan) the action authorized has been entirely inadequate to address the problem.

Every failure of the UN in the 1990s—and these were many: Rwanda, Croatia, Bosnia, Kosovo (in which NATO intervention took place without UN Security Council authorization) and elsewhere—occurred because the idealistic aspirations of security cooperation could not be translated into action and could not supplant diverging state interests. In Rwanda, the UN hierarchy in New York ignored the warnings of its commander on the ground that genocide was imminent. This happened partly because of bureaucratic inertia and partly because of stagnation within the organization. It is a sad reality that Rwanda also occurred because the major powers did not regard events at the time as affecting their vital interests and because they underestimated the dangers to the civilian population.

For most countries, the utility of the United Nations generally extends only as far as the organization is willing to support their interests and actions. At times the UN is, of course, of use to the major powers. For instance, the French found the UN Security Council useful in providing after-the-fact justification for their military intervention in the Ivory Coast in 2003. Similarly, the United States brought in the United Nations to sanction some of its policies in Iraq after it had already occupied the country.

Yet, for the United States, the events of the 1990s, and particularly the failure of UN Security Council members to support the American/British invasion of Iraq in 2003 (an action that served to implement long-standing Security Council resolutions on Iraq), diminished the utility and importance of the UN in American foreign policy. President Bush had declared that the UN faced a major "test" on the issue of Iraq and in the view of the administration, and many other Americans, it failed that test rather decisively. As the president commented in Canada in 2004, "the success of multilateralism is measured not merely by following a process, but by achieving results. The objective of the UN and other institutions must be collective security, not endless debate."[17] Some in Canada have also recognized this. As Opposition Leader Stephen Harper noted during the debate on whether Canada should participate in the Iraq campaign: "The limits of UN declarations are not the limits of Canadian foreign policy or our security needs."[18]

But most Canadians have not yet faced the reality of what the UN is and what it is not. While the government of Canada has become an advocate of UN reform, the United Nations cannot act as the supranational organization that many Canadians envisage. Indeed, reforms that are currently proposed, whether increasing the size of the Security Council or adding more permanent members[19], will not alter the fact that the UN is composed of sovereign states that will always have fundamental interest and policy differences. Indeed, such reforms would likely compound those problems.

The Question of Legitimacy

At its 60th anniversary summit in September 2005, in a blistering speech about the failure of its ambitious reform plan heavily pushed by Canada, Prime Minister Martin nevertheless said that, "Canada cannot conceive of the world succeeding without the United Nations."[20] The notion that the success of the world depends on the UN is a rather frightening prospect. But as we have already seen, it is also certainly, and fortunately, false.

But a primary reason that the United Nations cannot function as envisaged is that it is not the source of moral authority that many Canadians believe it to be. As posited by Prime Minister Martin, if the UN doesn't work for all (i.e., the North Koreas, Syrias, and Irans of the world), and promote their objectives, then it cannot work at all. This line of thinking is what the former Israeli ambassador to the UN, Dore Gold, calls the "ideology of impartiality" that now pervades the organization,[21] and, indeed, Canadian thinking. It is an ideology that is fundamentally at odds with the values of the Canadians who originally helped found the organization.

When the United Nations was founded, most member states were democracies. However, in the late 1940s, when the communist powers blocked the UN from functioning as had been intended, Canada and other western states were quite prepared to operate outside the UN as necessary. Indeed, this is exactly what they did when they founded NATO in 1949.

Today fewer than half of the UN's member states are democracies and this leads to some egregious situations. For instance, because all UN member states tend to take their turn on the UN's various committees and commissions, some of the worst human rights abusers, countries such as Cuba, North Korea, Syria, the Republic of the Congo, Egypt, Nigeria, Saudi Arabia, and Zimbabwe have all sat on the UN Human Rights Commission in the past decade. That commission was actually chaired by Libya in 2003.[22] There is a larger problem of serious corruption at the UN, which partly flows from the undemocratic culture that characterizes many of the member states.[23]

With respect to international security, many Canadians believe that only the UN Security Council can legitimize the use of force by states. Yet the Security Council is really no more than a committee of governments, some of which are often very unsavory and/or hostile to Western interests. In that context, the moral authority alleged to be imparted by the Security Council's sanction of a particular military action is, at best, limited.

Despite this, many Canadians continue to believe that the UN is the source of moral authority for Canadian security actions overseas. For instance, Jennifer Welsh argues that Canada should use military force only under three scenarios: In cases of self-defence, as outlined in Article 51 of the UN Charter; as a collective peace enforcement mission authorized by the UN; and in extreme humanitarian emergency or gross violations of human rights. "The use of force" in other circumstances she argues, such as "to overturn a regime or government without justifiable cause (that is, one of the three conditions listed above) is both illegal and immoral." This "illegality", she asserts, was the case in Iraq.[24]

But how is this to be judged and by whom? Under Jennifer Welsh's own criteria, the Iraq war is easily justified as a "humanitarian emergency", not requiring UN approval, since the number of dead at the hands of the Saddam Hussein regime exceeded those in Kosovo many times over. In Kosovo in 1999, Canada participated in a war that had no specific UN Security Council authorization.

Moreover, the interpretation of Article 51 of the UN Charter is highly subjective. A recent UN report suggests that states are entitled to take military action if a threatened attack is considered "imminent."[25] But again who is to judge this? In the final analysis, the interpretation of what constitutes self-defence and what encompasses imminent threat remains in the hands of individual states. Thus, in 2003, the United States was able to argue that in an age of weapons of mass destruction (WMD) it could not afford to take the risk that Iraq possessed such weapons. The fact that no WMD were found in Iraq is immaterial to the perception of threat.

Paul Heinbecker would suggest that such thinking threatens to return the world to the "law of the jungle." "Few outside the ambit of American exceptionalists," he said, "doubt that the rule of law is preferable to the law of the jungle ...."[26]

However, it is not so-called American exceptionalists who stand in the way of the UN realizing the ideals of its founders; rather, it is the reality that 191 sovereign states have diverse interests and at times will use force to protect their vital interests. Whether sanctioned by the UN Security Council or not, the interpretation as to when the use of force is justified will always be highly subjective. The ability of a state to use force or go to war has much less to do with international law or the Charter of the United Nations as it does with the realities of how power is dispersed in the international system.

A more realistic international policy would begin to view the United Nations as a tool like any other. At times it may be a valuable tool. But the organization is really no more than the sum of its parts. Owing to its makeup and because of the primary obligation that democratic countries have to their own people, it cannot be the primary source of moral authority for Canada. Where the UN is incapable of supporting Canadian interests, it should not be permitted to exercise a veto over the conduct of Canadian international policy.

Toward a Hard-Headed International Policy

The challenges outlined in the previous three chapters cannot be met unless they are recognized. For that to happen, we must realize that our current ideological approach has resulted in an increasingly impotent international policy that is insufficiently cognizant of the strategic, economic, and political realities that confront Canada. This has led to a dead end; practically to a kind of *de facto* protectorate status.

The myths that lie at the core of current policy are an impediment to the adoption of a policy that is both effective and represents the interests of the Canadian people. In the place of an ideological approach, a more effective international policy must be based the following premises. These include the recognition that:

1. Canada and the United States share common core values and the essentially same strategic interests.
2. Canadian international policy objectives must be based on the realities of the international system as it is, not as some might wish it to be.
3. Canadian diplomatic policies must attempt to achieve results that strengthen Canada's reputation, influence, and credibility with those countries that matter most to us, particularly the United States.
4. Canadian objectives in international policy must advance the collective political, economic, and security interests of the Canadian people, not the partisan interests of particular parties and leaders.
5. Canada must focus its political, financial, and military efforts on pursuing those interests deemed most important to the nation.
6. Canada should view multilateralism as a tool of foreign policy, not a source of moral authority; that true moral authority for Canadian foreign policy actions flows from the consent of the Canadian people.

Changing the way we think about such facts also requires changing the way we think institutionally. For various reasons our government and political institutions have not fostered the frank debate needed not only to answer important questions but to even recognize their importance. Thus, a related imperative for real policy reform is to move from a weak-state approach to a strong-state approach in making foreign policy. We must improve the ability of national political institutions to represent the real interests of Canadians in the making of international policy. But first, let us examine how the deterioration of our foreign policy assets, which has occurred under the influence of our unfortunate national myths, has undermined our capacity to carry out not merely a reinvigorated traditional diplomacy but also the new values-based variety.

—NOTES—

[1] Statement by Prime Minister Jean Chrétien in Support of a Motion in the House of Commons, April 8, 2003, Former Prime Minister's Newsroom

Archives (1995–2003), Privy Council Office, [http://www.pco-bcp.gc.ca/
default.asp?Language=E&Page=pmarchive&Sub=Speeches&Doc=
statementoniraq.20030408_e.htm]

[2] Major-General Natynczyk was a deputy commander of US III Corps in
Baghdad. General Natynczyk's official biography states: "In January 2004, he
deployed with III Corps in support of Operation Iraqi Freedom to Baghdad, Iraq,
serving first as the Deputy Director of Strategy, Policy and Plans and subsequently
as the Deputy Commanding General of the Multi-National Corps Iraq." [see:
http://www.forces.gc.ca/dsa/app_bio/engraph/FSeniorOfficerBiographyView_e.asp?
SectChoice=1&mAction=View&mBiographyID=307]

[3] Interview

[4] *Canada's International Policy Statement: A Role of Pride and Influence in the
World* Overview Paper (2005) p. 26.

[5] *Canada's International Policy Statement: A Role of Pride and Influence in the
World* Overview Paper (2005) p. 26.

[6] CTV News story online (April 18, 2005).

[7] Privy Council Office. Report of the International Policy Framework Task
Force, *Toward an International Policy Framework for the 21st Century* (July 2003)
p. ii

[8] Some continue to argue that international organizations, such as the UN and
NATO can fulfill such a counterbalancing role, but such arguments often draw
on Cold War, rather than post-Cold War, arguments and examples in making
that case. Both institutions are rather weak to fulfill such a role. For such an
argument see Thomas Axworthy, "Unwilling to be Willing: The Primacy and
Capability Principles in Canadian American Relations" (A Paper prepared for the
Canadian Defence and Foreign Affairs Institute. May 2003) p. 6

[9] William Hogg, "Plus ça Change: Continuity, Change and Culture in Foreign
Policy White Papers" *Intêrnational Journal* LIX (Summer 2004): 521–536

[10] Privy Council Office, *Toward an International Policy Framework for the 21st
Century* (July 2003) p. 12

[11] See: Douglas Bland, "Canada and Military Coalitions: Where, How and with
Whom?" in Hugh Segal ed. *Geopolitical Integrity* (Montreal: IRPP, 2005) p. 119

[12] Paul Heinbecker, "The UN in the Twenty-First Century" in David Carment,
Fen Osler Hampson and Norman Hillmer, *Canada Among Nations 2004:
Setting Priorities Straight* (Montreal/Kingston: McGill-Queen's University Press,
2005) p. 252

[13] Canada. *Canada in the World: Canadian Foreign Policy Review* (1995) Chapter Four

[14] *Canada's International Policy Statement: A Role of Pride and Influence in the World,* Diplomacy Paper (2005) p. 20

[15] Prime Minister's Office, "Prime Minister Paul Martin speaks at the World Economic Forum on 'The Future of Global Interdependence'" (January 23, 2004).

[16] Romeo Dallaire, *Shake Hands with the Devil: The Failure of Humanity in Rwanda,* (Vintage Canada, 2004) p. 520

[17] United States. White House, "President Discusses Strong Relationship with Canada", (Speech in Halifax, December 1, 2004)

[18] House of Commons, Hansard, (October 1, 2002) 37th Parliament. Second Session. Comments at 19:10 Minutes.

[19] United Nations, High-Level Panel on Threats, Challenges and Change, *A More Secure World: Our Shared Responsibility* (2004) pp. 66–69

[20] Prime Minister's Office, *Address by Prime Minister Paul Martin at the United Nations General Assembly,* (September 16, 2005 New York, New York) [See: http://www.pm.gc.ca/eng/news.asp?id=584]

[21] Dore Gold, *Tower of Babble: How the United Nations has fueled Global Chaos,* (Dore Gold Books, 2004) pp. 135–154

[22] Dore Gold, *Tower of Babble,* pp. 31 and 192

[23] A notable example is the corruption in the UN's oil for food program in Iraq in the 1990s, a scandal which also sucked in high ranking Canadians serving at the UN. See for instance, Steven Edwards "Saddam Bilked UN of $21 billion" *National Post* (November 17, 2004); "Frechette's Failings" *Ottawa Citizen* (September 9, 2005); Shawn McCarthy "Strong Took Tainted Cheque, Inquiry Finds" *Globe and Mail* (September 8, 2005)

[24] Jennifer Welsh, *At Home in the World: Canada's Global Vision for the 21st Century* (Toronto: Harper Collins, 2004) p. 40

[25] United Nations, High-Level Panel on Threats, Challenges and Change, *A More Secure World: Our Shared Responsibility* (2004) p. 4

[26] Paul Heinbecher, "The UN in the Twenty-First Century" *Canada Among Nations 2004* p.252

CHAPTER 5

The Erosion of National Capabilities

T he absence of strong strategic policy direction was the number one concern raised by departments during the Task Force consultations. Without this direction, departments lack a clear vision of Canada's role in the world, its key interests and its policy priorities.

–Privy Council Office Task Force Internal Report, Toward an International Policy Framework for the 21st Century, July 2003

In 2005, famine hit Niger after drought and locusts devastated crops in West Africa in 2004. The international response was slow and by July 2005, some three million people—more than one-quarter of Niger's population—were in danger of starvation.[1]

Just a few months earlier, the Canadian government had announced that Niger would be one of our 25 new "principal development partners." It seemed natural to expect Canada take a lead role in providing urgent humanitarian assistance. And by August our government had promised $10 million for food and medical aid, and to help ensure long-term food self-sufficiency.[2] Unfortunately the need was immediate and Canada's ability to deliver and distribute aid rapidly was virtually non-existent. Old-fashioned military lift capacity, *not* networking in international organizations, was needed, and we didn't have it.

A few months later, another of Canada's "principal development partners", Pakistan this time, was also in need. On this occasion, while the Disaster Assistance Response Team (DART) was dispatched, airlift was again a problem. The DART had to wait for ten days until leased heavy-lift aircraft arrived from the former Soviet Union to move them. (In contrast, British heavy-lift aircraft had both aid and transport helicopters in Pakistan within a few days).

The two events exposed serious gaps between Canada's declaratory policy and its real capabilities. The idea of a global Canadian role is central in Canadian policy but is particularly undermined by the poor state of the country's airlift capacity. The Canadian Forces' airlift capacity consists, theoretically, of 32 medium-sized C-130 "Hercules" cargo planes capable of carrying outsized cargo. But owing to the age of the airframes (two-thirds are more than 30 years old), only 13 of these aircraft are "mission-ready" at any given time.[3] In both East Timor in 1999 and Haiti in 2004, the aircraft that were assigned suffered breakdowns that interrupted the missions. The Canadian Forces also have no medium-lift helicopters to move troops and materiel once they are "in-theatre." In terms of heavy-lift capacity for moving larger quantities of supplies, heavy vehicles, or large helicopters, there is none.

While the previous government initiated a process to acquire 16 new medium-lift aircraft, it will likely be well into 2006 before a contract can be placed. Until the election of the Harper government, there were no plans to acquire national heavy-lift capacity, which would seem to be one essential prerequisite for a real global role.

The lack of such assets restricts the ability to even do humanitarian work. When a disaster is accompanied by civil unrest or war, an effective response requires far more substantial capabilities. They include not only robust combat forces but the vastly greater logistical support, strong national intelligence assets, and effective and informed command and control. Even though the Martin government has made global "nation-building" a cornerstone of Canadian international policy, all those capabilities are lacking.

And what about disasters within Canada? The ability to respond to domestic emergencies is the backbone of national sovereignty. Yet during the 1997 Manitoba flood and the 1998 ice storm, American transport aircraft had to be brought in to lift Canadian troops and supplies to affected Canadian regions. Half a decade later, the Senate Committee on National Security and Defence estimated in 2002 that it would take "days rather than hours" to move DART from bases in central Canada to a major disaster on the east or west coast.[4] After 9/11, when the Canadian Forces were called upon to move emergency supplies to Newfoundland for the thousands of air passengers who were diverted to Canada, there was simply no air transport available for the job.[5] It shouldn't have come as a surprise.

National capabilities essentially fall into three categories, the so-called "3 Ds" of diplomacy, development, and defence. To this should be added national intelligence capability but Canada doesn't have a foreign intelligence service. This chapter discusses what is a growing gap between declaratory policy and actual capabilities: a gap that increasingly makes declaratory policy rather hollow.

Diplomacy

The biggest problem with Canadian diplomatic policy is an absence of clear focus. This is the product of a consistent failure to clearly define the national interest. In its "Report on Plans and Priorities" (RPP) for 2005–2006, the Department of Foreign Affairs outlines nine policy priorities for Canada's diplomatic policy.[6] The International Policy Statement released in April 2005, in turn, had several broad diplomatic priorities:

- Fostering the North American Partnership by supporting the revitalization of our partnership with the United States and expanding cooperation with Mexico, exploring trilateral initiatives and devoting renewed attention to the Arctic;
- Making a distinctive contribution to Canada's efforts to help build a more secure world, in particular with regard to failed and failing states, counterterrorism and organized crime, the proliferation of weapons of mass destruction and human security;
- Promoting a new multilateralism that emphasizes global responsibilities, and a reformed multilateral system that tackles major global issues, including the environment, and health, by putting results ahead of process;
- Realigning bilateral relationships and building new networks (beyond North America) key to both our interests and values, taking into account the rise of major new players.[7]

Under this framework, countries, regions, and issues declared to be important included: the United States, Mexico, China, India, Brazil, sub-Saharan Africa, Afghanistan, Pakistan, the Middle East, Europe, Russia, the Ukraine, Japan, Latin America, the United Nations, other international organizations, and any potential failed or failing state. While some argue that North America and the United States were *de facto* priorities within the government's policy declarations, depending on the circumstances so, too, was nearly everything else.

As shown in Table 5, a certain sense of Canada's *de facto* diplomatic priorities can perhaps be gleaned from identifying the ten largest diplomatic missions.

Table 5: Ten Largest Canadian Diplomatic Posts Abroad, January 2005

Mission	Foreign Affairs Employees	Other Government Employees	Total
Embassy Washington D.C.	52	11	63
Embassy Beijing	27	20	47
High Commission New Delhi	18	26	44
Embassy Paris	30	14	44
High Commission London	28	14	42
Embassy Tokyo	32	6	38
Embassy Moscow	21	13	34
Mission Geneva (UN/World Trade Organization)	20	8	28
Embassy Manila	12	15	27
Embassy Berlin	20	5	25

Source: Department of Foreign Affairs, Ottawa

It is faintly reassuring that the embassy in Washington is the largest. But are 63 staff members in total really sufficient given the centrality of this relationship to Canada? Note that Berlin and Paris combined have 69 staff; yet, while Germany and France are important in world affairs, their significance to Canada pales in comparison with the United States. About 2.5 percent of our trade is with Germany and France combined vs. 75 percent with the U.S. And 71 people total are assigned to New Delhi and Manila. The high proportion of "other departmental staff" is probably linked to Canada's immigration policy, but India accounts for 0.29 percent of our trade; the Philippines, 0.18 percent.[8]

Even adding the 73 or so staff assigned to Canada's various consulates around the United States, only about 9 percent of Canadian diplomats and other departmental staff abroad are assigned to the country that dominates nearly every aspect of our international relations.[9] And at Foreign Affairs headquarters in Ottawa in the recent past, the Canada-U.S. relations division has often had fewer staff officers than were tasked to support various departmental human security initiatives.[10] While raw numbers cannot tell the whole story, they indicate a dispersal of scarce diplomatic resources to marginal policy objectives at the expense of what really matters.

On a day to day basis, it is true, the Canada-U.S. relationship largely "runs itself" through extensive cross border links between many federal departments and their U.S. counterparts, between provinces and states, and at the local and private levels. But the complexity and importance of the relationship, and the need to monitor and manage it carefully, does not afford the Department of Foreign Affairs the luxury of dispersing its attention on a wide-variety of initiatives around the world. In this regard Derek Burney comments that "No amount of new resources can offset the deleterious effect of a lack of commitment or sense of purpose by the Prime Minister and his senior Ministers in managing relations with Washington."[11] While the IPS now acknowledges that the Canada-U.S. relationship was the "anchor" of Canada's international policy, former deputy prime minister John Manley recently said: "I defy you to find any minister, either foreign affairs or trade or even any deputy minister, who invests time and effort in the Canada/U.S. relationship to a degree that is at all commensurate with its importance to the economy."[12]

There are other problems as well. Given the vast number of activities in which Foreign Affairs Canada (FAC) is engaged, there is little sense of in-depth policy expertise. Foreign service officers are not hired for specific or in-depth knowledge. They are policy generalists who often spend a few years in one area and then move on to another part of the world. For a country with a declaratory nation-building agenda that requires both focus and long-term, in-depth, knowledge and commitment, this is bizarre to be sure.

It starts to become almost surreal when one realizes that Canada has no foreign intelligence service. While the Communications Security

Establishment (CSE), which carries out electronic intelligence, has reportedly been used to assist some of our international trade negotiations, and perhaps other activities,[13] the lack of a dedicated national intelligence service forces us to rely almost exclusively on our diplomatic missions overseas. This is a hit and miss proposition.

For example, when Canada embarked on its 1996 Zaire adventure, there was no Canadian diplomatic mission either in that country or in neighbouring Rwanda. These countries were simply not of major concern for Canadian foreign policy.[14] Similarly, when Canadian troops went to Afghanistan in 2003, a Canadian embassy had to be hurriedly opened. The Foreign Affairs department had little real knowledge about Afghanistan and no substantive contacts with major political figures there. By 2005, our embassy there still had only six staff.[15] And yet Afghanistan is the largest recipient of Canadian aid, and more Canadian troops are deployed there than anywhere else.

This situation is far from atypical. In early 2005, the Department of Foreign Affairs and International Trade had about 965 employees dispersed among 151 diplomatic missions abroad.[16] Missions range from one person in a particular consulate to about 50 FAC personnel at the Canadian embassy in Washington. Other government departments have also assigned, in total, about 500 employees to Canadian missions abroad, distributed according to where there are international policy issues relevant to that department.

Analysts who have looked at the state of Canada's diplomatic service have pointed to another serious problem. Andrew Cohen notes how the sharp reduction of resources in the 1990s sapped the morale of Foreign Affairs,[17] as it became nearly impossible for the country to be credible on the international stage. Since foreign policy is often regarded as a discretionary activity by some politicians, it has also often been the first department to be cut in hard times.

The IPS itself discussed some of these resource-related issues. It acknowledged, for example, that Australia maintains 12 trade offices in China against Canada's 8, half actually contracted and operated by the Canada-China Business Council. It also pointed out that Australia spends three times as much per officer on language training as Canada, while New Zealand spends almost nine times as much.[18] But resources are not the only, or even the major, problem. Instead, these contrasts illustrate the essential difference between focused and unfocused policy. Both

Australia and New Zealand concentrate on the Asian and South Pacific regions, which naturally enables them to focus resources much more effectively, and to support the development of real policy expertise.

The conduct of a "global foreign policy", even a symbolic one, borders on the ridiculous when resources are as limited as they are in Canada. The budget for the Department of Foreign Affairs totals about $1.8 billion, of which $1.15 billion, or 64 percent in 2005, was soaked up by basic operating and capital expenses, and by contributions to employee benefit plans. Grants and contributions to international organizations consume most of the rest.[19] All told, it averages only $10 million per country, which isn't much considering the ambitious range of activities currently supported, at least rhetorically. Yet it is enviable by comparison with the state of our armed forces.

Defence

Canada's defence policy today is confronted by three principal challenges. The first involves the progressive decline in the core capabilities of the Canadian Forces, a process that is now well advanced. The second involves the need to completely transform the armed forces to respond to the rapid technological change that is occurring in military technology—what has sometimes been called "the revolution in military affairs." The third, and most fundamental, challenge is Canada's growing military dependence on the United States. This has largely emerged as a result of Canadian policy choices (or failures to choose), and is bringing Canadian and American security policies closer together, but in the context of fewer independent options for Canada.

The Decline of Core Capabilities

Over the past decade, Canadian military capabilities have declined sharply. Troop levels have fallen from about 78,000 to about 60,000 (of whom fewer than 55,000 are "trained effectives"). The regular army has a field force of only about 9,000 soldiers. Jet combat aircraft are down from about 170 to only 80. Two-thirds of the air transport fleet is over 30 years old, and their operational availability is about 50 percent and declining. The navy, at present in the best shape of the three services, faces significant re-equipment challenges in the near future.

The combination of a 30 percent real cut in defence budgets between 1993 and 1999, and more than a dozen major commitments over the past decade, have forced the military to continually borrow money from re-equipment programs to fund current operations. As noted in a recent study, *Canada Without Armed Forces?*, the force of the 1990s became the "unwitting enemy" of the future force in Canada, leading to a multi-faceted decline too steep to be reversed before certain capabilities fail entirely.[20] Many other Western countries managed to participate in missions during that decade while making prudent investments for the future. Once again, our lack of a "strategic culture" included not only an inability to relate means to ends, but a comprehensive failure to grasp the necessity of trying to do so.

Many current core systems are reaching the end of their effective service life faster than they can be replaced. Defence analyst Colonel (retired) Brian MacDonald recently called the resulting challenge "grim."[21] While the 2005 budget promised new funding for defence, it is far from clear if there will be sufficient funding to replace even existing core capabilities, let alone to acquire projected new ones, so vital to the transformation of the armed forces to meet the military challenges of the 21st century.[22]

In each of the service elements, air, ground, and naval, core capabilities are at risk of disappearing. Not all are glamorous; the army's aging fleet of trucks is often unreliable at home and abroad, and they carry expensive maintenance costs.[23] The army has also been unable to replace its mobile artillery (the M-109 self-propelled guns) or main battle tanks with equivalent modern systems. The operational consequence is the loss of mobile indirect fire support and heavy armour for forces deploying overseas.

But then the capacity to rapidly deploy operational forces overseas is also severely restricted. As already noted, only 13 of 32 C-130 transport aircraft are mission-ready at any given time. Nineteen of these aircraft (the "E" models) are 40 years old. They are the oldest C-130s flying anywhere in the world, and their operational availability, as of 2003, was only about 47 percent. The 13 remaining "H" model C-130s (4 of them over 30 years old), were available only 55 percent of the time in 2003.[24] While the replacement of the older model C-130s is now a government priority, they may not be replaced before the turn of the decade, and on less than a one-for-one basis.[25]

The Canadian navy has very limited integral sealift. The navy's two operational support ships are more than 36 years old. While these two vessels can transport some army equipment, their primary tasking is to refuel and re-supply warships at sea.[26] The Joint Support Ship (JSS) is intended to replace the existing support ships, but none have been ordered yet, and the first is unlikely to arrive before 2012 at the earliest.[27] Some consideration is also being given to acquiring a real amphibious vessel/helicopter carrier type capability, but this is in its early stages and may not materialize for a decade or more—if indeed it ever does.[28]

Additional capabilities are also on their last legs. The navy's three air defence and command destroyers, at over 33 years old, are all well past their original life expectancy. Without the destroyers, no integral command and control capability (even for domestic operations) or long-range air defence protection exists. The previous government's Defence Policy Statement (DPS) and the Conservative Party's election defence plan have both called for a destroyer and frigate replacement vessel. Yet it is likely that the destroyers will be scrapped before their replacements arrive.[29]

Similar trends are observable with respect to the air force's combat capabilities. These now rest entirely on the CF-18 fighter aircraft and, while they are being modernized, total numbers have been cut to just 80, which means just 34 are mission-ready on any given day.[30] (One lonely CF-18 flew over the September 2005 inauguration of the new governor general.[31]) With the priority tasking of these aircraft for North American security, only six are likely to be available for future overseas deployments.

The Challenge of Defence Transformation

Warfare in the 21st century has changed, both politically and technologically. In addition to the challenges of eroding core capabilities, the armed forces must simultaneously engage in substantial, long-term investment of money to transform the Canadian Forces, and keep them relevant and interoperable with allied forces. Brigadier Lamont Kirkland, of NATO's Transformation Headquarters, says the hallmarks of military operations today and in the future are:

> truly integrated joint forces, accelerated decision making, and overmatching power, all resulting from the application of speed,

precision, knowledge and lethality and from relying heavily on precision firepower, special forces, psychological operations and networked communications.[32]

The Department of National Defence defines transformation as a "process of strategic re-orientation in response to anticipated or tangible change to the security environment, designed to shape a nation's armed forces to ensure their continued effectiveness and relevance."[33] As the DPS acknowledges, this "transformation" necessitates extensive investment in C4ISR (command, control, communications, computers, intelligence, surveillance, and reconnaissance) to create integrated joint forces. The costs of this transformation across all three services are potentially enormous since they involve a massive change, not only in weapons systems, but in training, doctrine, and operations. Moreover, rapid technological change means many capabilities will have to be replaced much more frequently than they have been historically if the Canadian Forces are to remain up-to-date.

The army is currently leading the transformation process, moving toward a light- to medium-weight high-tech, digitized force able to operate effectively at home and in a variety of environments overseas. The army has, not unreasonably, given priority to high-tech equipment for the individual soldier, more lethal systems for light armoured vehicles, better tactical intelligence capabilities including unmanned air vehicles, and (finally) medium—weight transport helicopters (the latter two both vital for domestic emergencies).

Transformation will require organizational change and a greater number of personnel. Thus, the DPS of 2005 confirmed the goal of expanding the Forces' regular and reserve components by 5,000 and 3,000 personnel respectively. The Conservative defence plan is even more ambitious, calling for an additional 13,000 regulars and 10,000 more reserves. Under the DPS, a new command structure centered on a "Canada Command" has been established to improve their ability to defend Canada and North America—a goal described as the military's first priority.[34]

As Table 6 shows, today the army is able to "surge" and deploy a brigade headquarters and 2,000 troops for six months to one year (as in Afghanistan in 2003–04), but it cannot sustain such an effort over the long run. The DPS plans to expand this capacity, and by 2010, be able to deploy and sustain two task groups overseas, of up to 1,200 troops each, equipped with a range of new high-tech weapons and equipment.

However, it is uncertain that the Canadian Forces can meet its ambitious recruitment targets. It not only has to find the right mix of people for the high-tech force that is to come, but it must also add up to 13,000 net troops to the regular force, even as it will need to replace many of the 25,000 personnel who will reach their 20-year retirement dates between 2005 and 2011.[35]

Table 6: Deployable Canadian Combat Forces, 1994, 2006, and 2010 (Planned)

	1994	2006	2010 (Planned)
Special Forces	JTF2 plus Airborne Regiment (c. 900 men)	Special Operations Command (JTF2 plus special aviation and other elements)	Special Ops. Command, plus Special Ops. Regiment
Army	Battalion group (1,200 troops) within 3 weeks; Brigade plus battalion group (6,000 troops) within 90 days for up to six months.	Brigade HQ plus two "Task Forces" (c. 2,000 troops) for up to one year (1,000+ troops sustainable indefinitely).	Brigade HQ plus three larger Task Forces deployable for six months to one year; two task forces (c. 2,400 troops?) sustainable indefinitely.
Air Force	One Fighter Wing (24- 48 CF18s)	6 CF18s with precision guided munitions (PGMs)	6 modernized CF18s with PGMs
Navy	Task Group (4 combatants and one support ship) plus "appropriate" maritime air (Auroras)	Task Group (4 combatants) plus 2 Auroras for up to six months	Task Group plus 2 Auroras for up to six months (dubious without integral command destroyer).

Source: 1994 White Paper on Defence (p. 38–39); Defence Policy Statement (2005) p. 29–30.

Some, such as retired army colonel Howard Marsh, intimately involved in defence planning for decades, have argued that expanding the forces must be accompanied by sharp reductions in headquarters positions in favour of more troops at the sharp end.[36] Detailed analyses of personnel problems in the Canadian Forces suggest that the force currently envisaged will be too small for its projected tasks; Carleton University defence analyst Christopher Ankerson estimates existing tasks require closer to 85,000 troops.[37] This suggests that some global ambitions will have to be discarded in favour of meeting priorities closer to home.

A procurement process that is all too often too sluggish and at times too political, has also been a perennial problem. Most infamously, this led to a 20 year process simply to make a decision on new maritime helicopters. (These will now hopefully be delivered beginning in about 2009, and will replace ageing Sea Kings which, by that time, will be nearly 45 years old.) But streamlining bureaucracy and making the system more effective has habitually proven easier to say than to do.[38] All in all, there are significant challenges ahead as the government attempts to transform the Forces.

Military Dependence on the United States

The combined impact of eroding core capabilities and defence transformation is causing Canada to become more militarily dependent on the United States. While official Canadian rhetoric stresses the need for Canada to be an independent player on the world stage, the previous government did not support those declaratory aspirations with a consistent investment. For instance, the 1995 Foreign Policy White Paper proclaimed that "Canada is leading ... a ground-breaking study of options for a UN rapid reaction capability."[39] It has yet to materialize.

While many Canadians still see themselves as "the world's peacekeeper", to borrow a phrase from the CBC's Web site[40], Canada's international missions rarely correspond to what many believe this means. Early in 2005, 85 percent of Canadian troops deployed overseas were serving on *U.S.-led* rather than on UN-led missions. Only about 230 Canadian soldiers (or 15 percent of troops deployed) were engaged in purely UN missions; and more than 80 percent of these were deployed on the 30-year old mission on the Golan Heights. Most of these deployments are observer missions of between one and eight personnel.

The most important "peacekeeping missions" of recent years, Bosnia (after 1995), Kosovo, and Afghanistan, were actually all "coalitions of the willing", assembled under American leadership.[41] They were really more akin to imperial policing of the 19th century than what we think of as "peacekeeping", and they required robust combat capabilities. Since 9/11 in particular, these are operations that serve both Canadian and American security interests. When engaged in a major mission overseas, it is in Canada's interest to pull its weight and to maximize its tactical autonomy and influence.

At present, however, such missions are impossible for Canada without American logistic and other support. Generally, the farther away from Canada's shores a mission is, the more crucial American concurrence and support becomes. When the Canadian army operated in Kandahar, Afghanistan, in 2002, all of its equipment was transported there on American aircraft, Canadian troops flew on missions in American helicopters, relied on American fire support, and even drove American-supplied vehicles. While it is certainly the case that Canada also often provides transport or other support to American and other coalition forces, the difference is that American logistical support for key Canadian operations is often a prerequisite for the operation even being launched.

Some of Canadian capability gaps will be addressed if the transformation goals of the DPS and the Conservative defence plan are implemented. But other gaps in capability are likely to remain, and new ones will emerge as equipment ages. The limited size of the Canadian Forces also imposes problems in certain specific areas. Because Canada's special operations unit—Joint Task Force 2—is only comprised of a few hundred personnel, and because the Canadian Forces lack many of the assets (heavy airlift, appropriate helicopters, offshore support, etc) held by larger military forces, JTF2 must usually operate and integrate closely with American forces for any major operations abroad.

Even the larger army formations—such as envisaged army task forces—will have to be capable of "plugging-in" to larger allied (usually American) formations for major operations overseas. Toward that end, the army is acquiring much of the same equipment as the U.S. army's medium-weight "Stryker brigades." The transition to a light all-wheeled force is driven by the desire to buy "made-in-North America" (General Motors) equipment. In this regard, it is ironic that the Canadian-built LAV III vehicles (and the Stryker family of vehicles that have followed) are a real success story in Canada's defence industry. Countries around the world have adopted the LAV III, while the U.S. Army is now procuring 2,000 Stryker vehicles. But in its enthusiasm for the LAV III, Canada has decided to build its entire army on the LAV III/Stryker family of vehicles. In the process, all tracked vehicles are being discarded and key capabilities, such as tanks and mobile artillery, are being lost.[42] Still other capabilities, such as attack helicopters, are evidently deemed unaffordable. The end result is that Canadian task forces will largely be light formations, requiring significant allied (usually American) support in any medium or high threat scenarios.

Similar trends are observable in the navy and air force. In the future, the air force only envisages deploying a maximum of six CF-18s overseas. These would presumably have to be merged into a larger U.S. squadron or wing for any large-scale operation.[43] In the navy, the integration of Canadian frigates into U.S. carrier groups is already common. And if the ability to deploy self-sustaining Canadian naval task groups becomes more limited, that dependency will be complete.[44]

Former U.S. ambassador Paul Cellucci once noted that: "There are probably no two countries that are more interoperable than Canada and the United States, whether in terms of intelligence, equipment, or personnel."[45] This raises alarm bells in Canada, and some analysts have expressed concerns about the level of integration between the Canadian and U.S. militaries.[46] But, ultimately, it is Canadian policy choices that have created this dependency.

The United States has continually urged Canada to devote more attention to its national defence. In March 2005, Paul Cellucci outlined several areas in which he believed Canada should consider concentrating its military modernization efforts. Included in this list was a recommendation that Canada acquire its own independent strategic airlift to "respond effectively to international crises."[47] The Canadian Air Force has made a major push for such capabilities as well, arguing that a continent-sized country with global foreign policy aspirations requires it.[48] Indeed, despite the army's move to an all-wheeled lighter force, in a practical sense, most of these new vehicles can still only be moved by sea or by heavy-lift aircraft.

Both the Chrétien and Martin governments rejected the acquisition of independent strategic airlift capacity, arguing that Canada could simply charter heavy-lift aircraft as needed, and at much lower cost than it takes to purchase them outright. But if a major natural or man-made disaster occurs within Canada, chartered aircraft are not necessarily available immediately. Instead, they will probably only arrive in one to three days— or even longer. (American aircraft may also not be immediately available.) Since the first hours of a disaster are crucial to getting supplies, heavy equipment, helicopters, and the like into the affected region, that does not seem to be good enough.

The Conservative defence plan of 2006 envisages the acquisition of at least 3 heavy-lift aircraft. Following through on this pledge is important since the unintended political consequence of such policy decisions is a Canadian indication that it is content to leave its defence to the United States in an emergency. In his recent memoir, Paul Cellucci comments:

> What would give a greater boost to Canadian sovereignty than spending enough to take care of its own defense? National security doesn't just happen. Someone has to pay for it. Those Canadians who imagined that they were protecting their national sovereignty by permitting the United States to take care of an increasing share of continental defense had the equation backwards.[49]

The ballistic missile defence decision of 2005 sends exactly such a signal. The erosion of military capabilities threatens to extend the perception that Canada is willing to abrogate its defence to the United States, and to include maritime and territorial security as well. Since 9/11, territorial surveillance has become increasingly important, yet the assets available to the Canadian Forces are very limited, especially as both the Canadian Coast Guard and navy fleets age.[50] Taking part in joint surveillance efforts is vital to provide us with a *de facto* and *de jure* presence. It should not be a task that it largely left to the Americans alone.[51]

In general, past Canadian leaders have simply failed to understand that power and national capabilities are important instruments of sovereignty and international influence; that there is a cumulative consequence that accrues from chronic neglect. They have continued to act as though Canada is a fireproof house, and that both influence and sovereignty can be taken for granted. What Canadians should be concerned about is that the United States does not share this perspective.

Trends far deeper than most Canadians realize make further integration with the U.S. military a certainty. This is not necessarily a bad thing, but Canada should endeavour to ensure that such integration occurs under the most favorable circumstances and in a way that maximizes Canada's influence and capacity for independent action, particularly within the national territory. Credible policies, focusing on national-interest driven priorities, and appropriate funding levels are important levers for affecting the nature of integration and the level of Canadian dependency. At present, the capability trend of the Canadian Forces continues to decrease. Only a concerted effort will alter that trend.

International Aid

The primary purpose of Canadian aid policy over past decades has been to support global development in the world's poorest countries. As one CIDA (Canadian International Development Agency) document from 2000 notes:

> Canada's Official Development Assistance program supports sustainable development in developing countries in order to reduce poverty and to contribute to a more secure, equitable, and prosperous world.[52]

CIDA therefore advances policy objectives distinct from those pursued by the departments of Foreign Affairs and Defence but congruent with the international development community. It is largely politics at the United Nations that frames the nature of Canadian aid policy. Central to this approach is the "Millennium Declaration" agreed to at the UN's "Millennium Summit" in September 2000.

The Millennium Declaration, later refined through a "roadmap" produced by the UN Secretary General on September 6, 2001, contains a series of goals and targets. The goals, meant to be achieved by 2015, are:

1. The eradication of extreme poverty and hunger by halving the proportion of people suffering from hunger.
2. Ensuring that children everywhere will be able to complete a full

course of primary schooling.

3. Eliminating gender disparity in primary and secondary schooling.
4. Reducing the under-five mortality rate by two-thirds.
5. Reducing the maternal mortality ratio by three-quarters.
6. Halt and begun to reverse the spread of HIV/AIDS, malaria and other major diseases.
7. Halve the proportion of people without sustainable access to safe drinking water and basic sanitation and significantly improve, by 2020, the lives of at least 100 million slum dwellers.
8. Develop a global partnership for development with an open, rule-based, predictable, non-discriminatory trading and financial system while addressing many of the specific problems and needs of different categories of developing countries.[53]

These objectives are admirable but they are also highly idealistic since they seek to address issues that are beyond the control of any single nation or even a large group of nations. They result from political compromises between states and, in that sense, are artificial. The commitment of certain states to some of them—eliminating gender disparity in schooling to name one—are probably disingenuous. And the timetable, in particular, is probably one that cannot be met. The UN's 2005 *Human Development Report* comments that:

> Most countries are off track for most of the MDGs [Millennium Development Goals]" ... If current trends continue, there will be large gaps between MDG targets and outcomes.[54]

Yet, for Canada, the MDGs still "serve as an essential yardstick against which to assess our progress and target our efforts."[55] Indeed, Canadian interests are not a significant factor in the formulation of this country's aid policy. In this regard the IPS states:

> Canada's role in development cooperation cannot be defined exclusively on the basis of self-interest. The needs of our develop-

ment partners, first and foremost in the poorest countries, must be our starting point.[56]

What this really means is that when it comes to aid policy, the Canadian taxpayer has become a kind of cash cow funding overarching goals and objectives that are set outside of the government and the country, and are either extremely difficult to achieve or are, in fact, unachievable.

A Shotgun Approach to Aid Policy

In 2005, 155 states and territories in virtually all parts of the world received some form of Canadian assistance, spreading our $3.6 billion in development spending rather thinly. The IPS says 90 of those countries or territories received bilateral Canadian country-to-country assistance of less than $5 million a year, and 54 got less than $1 million.[57] Aid also goes to some dubious places. Many might also be surprised that countries like communist China (with an economy of $7.2 trillion[58]) and Vietnam are major recipients of Canadian aid—$54 million to the former in 2002–03, and $55 million to the latter.[59]

Leaving aside the issue of who gets Canadian aid for the moment, the Martin government declared that it planned to address the wide dispersal of aid resources by focusing assistance on 25 "core development partners." These core partners were named on April 19, 2005. As Table 7 notes, 14 are in Africa, 4 in the Americas, 6 in Asia, and 1 in Europe. But these states will not be the only recipients of Canadian aid. Indeed, only two-thirds of the bilateral portion of the aid budget (about $1.5 billion in 2005 dollars) will be allocated to them. Remaining bilateral and multilateral aid (totalling some $2.1 billion in 2005) will still go elsewhere. If divided evenly out of today's budget, each of Canada's principal aid partners would receive just under $60 million a year. This does not provide much in the way of real "focus."

Table 7: Canada's Trade, Aid, Economic, and Diplomatic Profile in States Identified as Core Development Partners

Country	Approximate Percentage of That State's Trade with Canada	Total Canadian Aid, 2002–2003 (in CDN million dollars)	Approximate Numbers of Canadian Diplomatic Staff in State
Niger	0.04	$15.52	1
Benin	0.22	$9.62	None
Burkina Faso	0.22	$27.89	3
Rwanda	0.23	$17.25	2
Ukraine	0.23	$20.51	9
Mali	0.26	$31.72	4
Malawi	0.27	$31.55	None
Kenya	0.29	$16.37	24
Cameroon	0.42	$48.77	5
Mozambique	0.44	$43.89	4
Zambia	0.45	$33.63	4
Bolivia	0.51	$18.58	2
Senegal	0.52	$28.19	10
Vietnam	0.62	$55.09	12
Ethiopia	0.66	$76.09	8
Tanzania	0.71	$41.46	8
Indonesia	0.75	$30.18	17
Honduras	0.78	$18.57	2
Sri Lanka	0.85	$14.95	10
Cambodia	1.14	$19.54	1
Ghana	1.35	$33.12	14
Nicaragua	1.49	$16.07	None
Pakistan	1.56	$62.46	18
Bangladesh	1.63	$71.07	12
Guyana	12.17	$10.54	5

Source: IMF, Direction of Trade Statistics Yearbook 2004 and CIDA, "Statistical Report on Official Development Assistance Fiscal Year 2002–03 pp. 37–44. GDP figures in: International Institute of Strategic Studies, *Military Balance 2004-05.* "Canadian diplomatic staff" totals include Foreign Affairs, other government employees in the embassy and consular staff. Source: Department of Foreign Affairs.

It is notable that some of the largest recipients of Canadian aid internationally were not identified as principal aid partners. Afghanistan, for example, actually the largest recipient of Canadian aid internationally ($122.3 million in 2002–03), home to the largest Canadian military presence abroad, prominently among the "least developed countries" in the world[60] and of vital security interest for the West, is not a principal aid partner. Neither is Haiti, a country within our hemisphere. It is one of the poorest nations on earth, long a subject of Canadian concern and indeed military intervention, and one, unlike most of Canada's principal aid partners, that actually does more than one percent of its trade (1.65 percent to be exact[61]) with Canada.

This leads one to wonder how Canada's principal aid partners were selected. Three criteria were officially enunciated as instrumental in the selection of the 25 principal development partners. First was the level of poverty, calculated on criteria such as life expectancy at birth, adult literacy, and GDP per capita. According to CIDA "only countries below $1,000 U.S. dollars in average per capita annual income would be considered." Second was the ability to use aid effectively, measured by economic management, policies for social inclusion and equity, and the state of public sector management and institutions. Third, was whether there was a sufficient Canadian presence in the country to "add value" to the aid efforts. The strength of historical and people-to-people links was declared important in this respect.[62] But these three criteria do not appear to explain the actual list.

As to the first, according to CIDA's own statistical information, 49 states fall into the category of "least developed countries" in the world. Thirteen of these have been identified as new Canadian partners. Of 22 other "low income countries", seven made our list. And of 39 "lower middle income" states, four are included.[63] The 25th country is the Ukraine, which fits none of these categories, with a per capita GDP of about $5,460 USD per year. Since Canada's partners come from all parts of the globe, it is unclear how the poverty criteria were used to include some states but not others. One can surmise that the process almost certainly became highly political, with the domestic political strengths of particular ethnic communities likely being an important factor.

The relevance of the second criterion is equally questionable. One is led to question whether many of the new "partners" (Mozambique and Ethiopia to name two) really possess "governance mechanisms" suitable to "using the aid allocated to them effectively." It also seems doubtful that others, Pakistan for instance, will aggressively pursue "policies for social inclusion and equity."

As far as the third criterion is concerned, it is not clear whether Canada has an economic profile with most of the principal partners to "add value" to aid efforts. With only one exception, no partner state does more than 1.63 percent of its trade with Canada. Indeed, 19 of the new development partners conduct less than one percent of their total trade with us, 11 of them less than one-half of one percent. Guyana is the sole exception, and choosing a few more states like it would have leant greater credibility to Canadian aid policy.

Canada's corresponding diplomatic and military profile with its partner states is also weak. In Africa, which will be the future focus of Canada's aid efforts, we only have about 100 diplomats working in an extremely diverse continent of 900 million people who speak up to 800 languages. It is likely that regardless of how much we spend there, our in-depth knowledge of strategic, political, economic, cultural, and social realities will inevitably remain cursory. Given the limited power projection capabilities of the Canadian Forces discussed earlier, we have almost no capacity to respond quickly to rapidly unfolding humanitarian or other disasters in partner countries. As former senior Canadian diplomat Louis Delvoie has noted, the size of a country's political, development, and military presence in a given country is central in determining its status and ability to shape events[64], and with most of the partners we have chosen, our presence is very small.

It is true that by 2010, our overall development assistance is projected to rise to some $5 billion, and the bilateral portion will also increase.[65] But even this larger amount will be fairly widely dispersed. In a place like Africa, that aid will remain unsupported by larger economic interests. Our total trade with Africa at $3.7 billion USD is just 0.76 percent of all our trade. More than 81 percent of it is with just four countries—Algeria, Nigeria, Equatorial Guinea (all oil exporters) and South Africa.[66] This does not create much of a base to lead true development. And should that not be what Canadian aid is all about?

The Effectiveness of Our Aid

In general, aid can be divided into two broad categories: "humanitarian aid", given to people in distress by individuals, organizations, or governments to relieve suffering; and "development aid", provided for long-term and permanent poverty alleviation. The latter can be distinguished from humanitarian aid in that it is targeted to creating the conditions and environment for economic transformation, rather than easing suffering in the short term.

Humanitarian assistance is something that should be provided at some level regardless of where the need may be. However, assisting in the process of development is a much more complicated process requiring both long-term commitment and the right conditions. In particular, Canada's interests (economic, political, and strategic) must be such that our "natural presence" is indeed sufficient to add value to development efforts. Because resources are limited, Canada should choose carefully where it becomes involved or else our aid will not be effective.

In general, our efforts to promote development have been less than impressive. Although Africa has been the focus of much aid for some time, in the past two decades, the number of Africans living in extreme poverty has almost doubled. The root cause, it is increasingly acknowledged, is not economic but political: an absence of stability, and poor or non-existent governance.[67] Worse, in many parts of the world including Africa, these problems have gotten worse in recent decades.

No matter how much money Canada spends, in certain parts of the world structural impediments (particularly political instability and armed conflict) are certain to be a serious impediment to long-term development. EU Council President, Jean-Claude Juncker recently remarked, "Even if countries are spending like we are ... if you are giving huge amounts of money, if you don't have stability in these countries, this is a total waste of money and you aren't really helping people."[68]

These impediments are enhanced when Canada's broader economic, political, and military presence in a given region or country is small. Development work in a highly volatile, even hostile, security situation (the so-called "three block war" involving often simultaneous humanitarian assistance and military operations) requires immense resources. Arguably, what it really requires are the economic and strategic interests that can sustain the prolonged development work that may be required over many decades. Our most successful development work is likely to occur where our strongest interests lie.

Among our "principal aid partners", the largest absolute level of

Canadian assistance is provided to Ethiopia. Aid totalled $76 million in 2002–03, about 0.9 percent of Ethiopia's total GDP.[69] Since Ethiopia is a country of some 73 million people, total Canadian aid per person was just over $1 a year. In Bangladesh, it averages about 50 cents per person per year; in Indonesia, about 12 to 13 cents per person per year. Canadian aid is inevitably more "humanitarian" than it is real "development." Our projects have assisted individuals and particular communities with humanitarian needs but the overall trend does not suggest the millennium goals will be met by 2015. In Ethiopia, nearly half of Canadian aid ($29.38 million) in 2002–03 was to alleviate malnutrition, hunger, and disease. In Bangladesh, the second largest aid recipient among our partner countries, $10 million of just over $71 million was allocated for the same purpose.[70] Such aid seeks to relieve immediate distress, a worthy cause. But it is highly questionable whether it can ever create the conditions for long-term economic growth.

Aid, in and of itself, is insufficient to create such conditions. It is trade that does that. Trade is the engine that will ultimately develop and expand a national economy, but Canada is a small player in trade terms with most of its partners. Although Canadian aid programs may have a long history in some states, this has not given rise to strong economic or trade links between Canada and these countries.

Tanzania and Senegal represent interesting examples in this regard. Canadian aid programs there stretch back for many decades. But just 0.71 percent of Tanzania's trade is with Canada, while our aid of about $46 million in 2003 constituted just 0.35 percent of Tanzania's GDP ($9.6 billion USD).[71] Tanzania's largest trading partners in the developed world are South Africa (7.8 percent), Japan (5.5 percent), the UK (4.75 percent), Germany (4.41 percent), and the Netherlands (3.81 percent).[72] These countries are in a much stronger position to facilitate development in Tanzania over the long-term by virtue of their deeper economic presence there. And, in fact, development assistance to Tanzania from Britain, Germany, and the Netherlands combined is six or seven times our own, the equivalent of over $300 million per year.[73]

Senegal, in turn, is Canada's leading trading partner among the Franco-African states identified as principal development partners. Yet only 0.52 percent of Senegal's trade is with Canada and our $28 million in aid in 2002–03 is just 0.35 percent of Senegal's GDP.[74] Senegal's principal trading partners in the West are France (20.8 percent), Italy (5.2

percent), Spain (4.5 percent), and the United States (2.7 percent). And of total foreign aid to Senegal in 2002 of some $320 million USD, the largest donors were France (about 19 percent), Japan (11 percent), and the United States (9 percent).[75] Canada's bilateral aid to Senegal was about four percent of the total.[76] Among our principal aid partners, only in Guyana does Canadian aid exceed one percent of that country's annual GDP.[77]

It is reasonably clear that assisting real long-term development, or aid effectiveness, has not been the most important criteria in selecting Canada's principal aid partners. Instead, the inertia of existing policy, the "ideology of the aid community" and domestic political factors have been the central criteria. This essentially involves doing things in the same way that they have always been done, but with more money. A May 2004 Briefing Paper from the Canadian Council for International Cooperation, a coalition of Canadian development NGOs, called for a massive and even "legislated" Canadian effort to "eradicate poverty" and implement the millennium development goals. It advocated increasing Canadian aid by 12 to 15 percent per year for a full decade and rejected any narrowing of Canadian aid to focus on fewer countries.[78]

Many continually call for Canada to spend 0.7 percent of its GDP on aid. This has become a kind of panacea for Canadian aid policy. But calls for massive spending increases in any policy area are usually fiscally unrealistic because they are unsustainable in the long-term. Often they are calls made for political expediency, and they usually avoid the hard choices that might actually lead to real policy effectiveness. To be effective, Canadian aid policy objectives, like defence policy objectives, have to be both practically effective and fiscally realistic.

However, just as domestic politics in Canada is said to have come to "trump security", politics also seems to trump the emergence of a more realistic development strategy. Indeed, Professor Denis Stairs of Dalhousie University argues that the primary purpose of the development section of the IPS was largely to cause "it's readers to think that something is happening that in fact is not...." [79] Political leaders are driven to pursue aid policies that correspond with the perceived wishes of particular ethnic communities and NGOs. In that sense, a widely dispersed aid policy has come to be seen as politically attractive to most of Canada's political parties, whether such a policy is realistic or not, whether it is effective in advancing Canadian interests or not, and whether it actually facilitates much real long-term development or not. Both Canadian taxpayers and those we need to help deserve better.

Toward a Realistic and Achievable Aid Policy

There have been two major problems with Canadian development aid. First, its wide geographic dispersal and the fact that it has little relation to Canadian interests, has reduced its impact. Second, because it is driven by its own unique objectives, it has not been coordinated with the diplomatic and military aspects of Canada's international policy.

While this lack of coordination may have been a virtue in the past when aid was intended more or less exclusively for humanitarian purposes, it is a major problem now that Canada has made assisting failed and failing states a cornerstone of its international policy. Carleton University professor David Carment has pointed out that Canada's "3D" (diplomacy, defence, and development) strategy "looks promising on paper" but "the concept must be fully incorporated into the decision-making and planning process of various departments."[80] This requires overarching policy coordination and the prolonged political attention that only comes from a perception that real interests (economic, political and strategic) are involved.

A more realistic aid policy would differentiate between *development* and *humanitarian* assistance. It would seek to concentrate Canada's *development* work on those states and regions where Canada can make a real difference, where governance mechanisms are viable and appropriate, and where our country's national interests could benefit from a consistent and effective aid effort. There appears to be some recognition of this in the Conservative 2006 election platform, which states that: "Foreign aid has been used for political purposes, not to ensure genuine development. We need to ensure that Canada's foreign policy reflects true Canadian values and advances Canada's national interests."[81]

In Africa, the concentration of part of Canada's aid policy on a minimum of 14 (and in practice probably more) states will remain largely unsupported by complementary diplomatic or military efforts. In addition, because there are no clear national interests at stake, currently projected spending increases in the aid budget will be vulnerable to domestic budgetary priorities that happen to prevail from year-to-year. This does not mean that Canada should "turn its back" on Africa, but it does mean acknowledging that other countries are probably better positioned to lead there with respect to development; that Canada is going to make a stronger contribution if it focuses instead on one or two key aspects of *humanitarian* work (such as channelling most support to fight HIV/AIDS for example) and supports other countries that have a more comprehensive presence on that continent.

A reorientation of aid in this way would begin the process of ensuring that it is effective and, like any other instrument of policy, serves a larger purpose—the national interest.

****

As in every other aspect of Canada's international policy, the absence of a serious strategic culture and suitably robust supporting institutions has led to fatuous policies and misdirections of effort. It doesn't have to be that way. It is possible to identify key interests, rank them, and pursue them through a hard-headed assessment of the means available and their suitability to these ends, including the importance of acquiring greater capabilities that, among other things, clearly can be afforded by a nation as rich as Canada. It all starts with a clear assessment of what the national interest requires.

But first, let us examine how three other small- and middle-ranking states have sought to define their national interests and relate ends to means in pursuit of it.

—NOTES—

[1] Oxfam News "3.6 Million Face Starvation in Niger if the World Does Not Respond" (July 21, 2005); Robyn Dixon "Food Aid Begins Flowing in Niger" *Los Angeles Times* (August 13, 2005).

[2] CIDA "Niger Humanitarian Relief: Food Crisis in Niger" [http://www.acdi-cida.gc.ca/CIDAWEB/webcountry.nsf/VLUDocEn/Niger-Humanitarianrelief].

[3] Canada. Air Force "The Aerospace Capability Framework" (Director General Air Force Development, 2003) Chapter 3 p. 45.

[4] Senate, Standing Committee on National Security and Defence, *For an Extra $130 Bucks ...* (November 2002) p. 67.

[5] underground royal commission interview with retired Colonel Howard Marsh.

[6] Canada. Treasury Board Secretariat "Report on Plans and Priorities, 2005–06, Foreign Affairs Canada" (2005). [http://www.tbs-sct.gc.ca/est-pre/20052006/FAC-AEC/FAC-AECr5601_e.asp#section1.3.5]

[7] Canada. Department of Foreign Affairs, *Canada's International Policy Statement–A Role of Pride and Influence in the World, Diplomacy* (2005) p. 2.

[8] International Monetary Fund, *Direction of Trade Statistics Yearbook 2004*, pp. 119–20.

[9] The contrast with other regions of the world is equally telling. For instance, an equal number of Foreign Affairs employees were assigned to Canadian embassies and high commissions in Cuba, Zimbabwe, South Africa, Kenya, Bangladesh, and Tanzania as were assigned to the Canadian embassy in Washington D.C. (The breakdown was: Havana 10, Harare 7, Pretoria 12, Nairobi 14, Dhak, 3, and Dar Es Salaam 4). It is difficult to argue that these countries collectively come close to equalling the importance of the United States in Canadian international policy. Source: Department of Foreign Affairs, Access to Information Request A-2004-00285.

[10] See Roy Rempel *The Chatter Box: An Insider's Account of the Irrelevance of Parliament in the Making of Canadian Foreign and Defence Policy* p. 137.

[11] D.H. Burney "Canada-US Relations: Promise Pending?" *In the Canadian Interest? Assessing Canada's International Policy Statement* (Canadian Defence and Foreign Affairs Institute, November 2005) p. 13

[12] John Manley, Speech delivery at the Canadian Institute for International Affairs Conference, Calgary, Alberta, (March 27, 2004).

[13] Martin Rudner, "Canada's Communications Security Establishment: From Cold War to Globalisation" (Norman Patterson School, Carleton University, Occasional Paper #22, 2000) p. 28.

[14] Interview Louis Delvoie, underground royal commission documentary, *Question of Honour*, Episode 4

[15] These comprised three Foreign Affairs employees and three from other departments. Source: Foreign Affairs Canada.

[16] Source: Department of Foreign Affairs, Access to Information Request A-2004-00285

[17] Andrew Cohen, *While Canada Slept: How We Lost Our Place in the World* (Toronto: McClelland and Stewart, 2003) pp. 135–38.

[18] Canada. Department of Foreign Affairs, *Canada's International Policy Statement–A Role of Pride and Influence in the World, Diplomacy* (2005) p. 30

and Commerce Paper p. 10.

[19] Canada. Treasury Board Secretariat "Report on Plans and Priorities, 2005–06, Foreign Affairs Canada" (2005) Section 3, Table 3 [http://www.tbs-sct.gc.ca/est-pre/20052006/FAC-AEC/FAC-AECr5603_e.asp#section3table3]

[20] Doug Bland ed., *Canada Without Armed Forces?* (Queen's School of Policy Studies/Conference of Defence Associations, December, 2003) p. xiii.

[21] Brian MacDonald, "Update: Canada Without Armed Forces? Chapter 2: The Capital and the Future Force Crisis" in Conference of Defence Associations, *Understanding the Crisis in Canadian Security and Defence* (Ottawa: CDAI, March 2005) pp. 34–42.

[22] See: David Rudd "Boosting Defence, the Canadian Way" *Commentary* (Toronto: Canadian Institute of Strategic Studies, February 2005); Stephen Throne "Canada's Military Hanging by Fiscal Thread" Canadian Press story (April 24, 2005).

[23] Howard Marsh, "Sensitivity Analysis of Canadian Defence Spending Value for Money—Cost of the Canadian Forces" in Conference of Defence Associations, *Understanding the Crisis in Canadian Security and Defence* (Ottawa: CDAI, March 2005) p. 30–31. The trucks are a "high priority" for replacement, but this may mean perhaps after 2010.

[24] Discussed in Roy Rempel, "Crisis in Canada's Air and Sea Transport Capability" *Defence Associations National Network News* X (Summer 2003): 8–11.

[25] The new aircraft likely to be acquired is the C-130J model. It seems likely that 19 C-130Es and the 4 oldest C-130H aircraft will be replaced by 16 C-130Js. See Brian MacDonald, "The Capital and Future Force Crisis" in Doug Bland ed. *Canada Without Armed Forces?* p. 43; David Pugliese, "Liberals Scramble to Replace Hercs Before Election" CanWest News Service (November 21, 2005).

[26] The operational support ships have about 400 "lane meters" of lift capacity (defined as a segment of surface area measuring 2.5 metres by 1 metre) between them. When one is in refit, that capacity is halved. Similarly, whenever a support ship is deployed overseas for sealift, either the Pacific or the Atlantic fleet has no integral refuelling and re-supply capability.

[27] The JSS does not provide an amphibious capability to land troops or supplies in hostile environments. Instead, there will likely be space for "plug and play" computer systems—used by a small Joint Force Headquarters—as well as an "expandable" health care facility and accommodations for a maximum of 210 people. See discussion by Roy Rempel "Briefing Note for the Minister Outlines Envisaged Capabilities of the Joint Support Ship (JSS)" *Defence Associations*

National Network News XI (Fall 2004): 24–28.

[28] See Chris Wattie "Critics Say DND Asks Too Much of Shipbuilders" *National Post* (October 26, 2005).

[29] As of 2005, the mooted arrival date of the first ships is 2017. Chris Wattie "Critics Say DND Asks Too Much of Shipbuilders" *National Post* (October 26, 2005)

[30] Canada. Air Force "The Aerospace Capability Framework" (Director General Air Force Development, 2003) Chapter 5 p. 6.

[31] *National Post* (September 28, 2005).

[32] Brigadier Lamont Kirkland, "The Role of NATO Transformation Headquarters" *General Sir William Otter Papers* (Toronto: Royal Canadian Military Institute: No. 2/04) p. 2.

[33] Cited by: Lt. General Ken Pennie, "Transforming Canada's Air Force: Vectors for the Future" *Canadian Military Journal* (Winter 2004–05): 40.

[34] Canada. Department of Foreign Affairs, *Canada's International Policy Statement–A Role of Pride and Influence in the World, Defence* (2005) p. 2.

[35] While 25,000 personnel were recruited to the Canadian Forces between 1984 and 1992, that in-take was only 11,000 new personnel between 1992 and 1999, creating a huge potential gap in experienced personnel in the Canadian Forces over the next several years as the older generation retires. See summary in Howie Marsh, "A Claxton Paper; Canada Without Armed Forces?" On Track (Conference of Defence Associations, Vol. 8, No. 1, December 2003): 9–13. Already in 2002, the Senate Standing Committee on Defence reported that 11 Canadian military occupational categories were at "critical" levels below strength; of these at least 8 were 10 percent or more below strength with insufficient trainees to recover within the next two years. Senate, Standing Committee on National Security and Defence, *For an Extra $130 Bucks ...* (November 2002) p. 113.

[36] Howard Marsh, "Sensitivity Analysis of Canadian Defence Spending Value for Money—Cost of the Canadian Forces" in Conference of Defence Associations, *Understanding the Crisis in Canadian Security and Defence* (Ottawa: CDAI, March 2005) p. 32.

[37] Christopher Ankerson, "The Personnel Crisis" in Doug Bland ed. *Canada Without Armed Forces?* pp. 55–81. A new Ankerson study also casts doubt on the possibility of meeting those recruiting goals; (*Globe and Mail* September 26, 2005).

[38] See discussion by Sharon Waymont Hobson "The Defence Policy Statement and Procurement" *In the Canadian Interest? Assessing Canada's International Policy Statement* (Canadian Defence and Foreign Affairs Institute, November 2005) pp. 91–96

[39] Canada. Department of Foreign Affairs and International Trade. *Canada in the World: Canadian Foreign Policy Review, 1995* Chapter Four.

[40] See: cbc.ca/news/background/cdnmilitary/worldspeacekeeper.html

[41] For a discussion of evolving American interest in peacekeeping in the 1990s, see Joel Sokolsky, *The Americanization of Peacekeeping: Implications for Canada* (Kingston: Centre for International Relations, Queen's University, 1997)

[42] The army envisages eventually procuring a new mobile artillery system, but probably not before the turn of the decade and only if the money for it can be found.

[43] Canadian CF-18 squadrons/flights are most easily interoperable with U.S. Navy and Marine Corps F-18 units. Among NATO European air forces, only the Spanish Air Force flies the F-18 fighter.

[44] The strong professional and bureaucratic interest of the Department of National Defence and the Canadian Forces in enhanced interoperability is discussed in: Danford W. Middlemiss and Denis Stairs "The Canadian Forces and the Doctrine of Interoperability: The Issues" in Hugh Segal ed. *Geopolitical Integrity* (Montreal: IRPP, 2005) pp. 151–81.

[45] Remarks by U.S. Ambassador Paul Cellucci, Conference of Defence Associations Seminar "Canada-U.S. Relations and the Role of the Canadian Forces" (Ottawa: March 3, 2005).

[46] See for example Michael Byers, "Canadian Armed Forces Under United States Command" *International Journal* LVIII (Winter 2002–03): 89–114.

[47] Remarks by U.S. Ambassador Paul Cellucci, Conference of Defence Associations Seminar "Canada-U.S. Relations and the Role of the Canadian Forces" (Ottawa: March 3, 2005).

[48] The recognition that Canada's strategic circumstances and its global international policy aspirations require heavy airlift capability goes back to at least the 1960s when the Pearson government examined the option of buying such aircraft to support the government's mobile force concept. However, cost factors and a sluggish decision-making process prevented the acquisition from moving forward.

[49] Paul Cellucci *Unquiet Diplomacy* (Toronto: Key Porter Books, 2005) p. 118

[50] See Senate report comments related to this issue. Senate. Standing Committee on National Security and Defence. *Canada's Coastlines: The Longest*

Under-Defended Borders in the World (October 2003).

[51] See for instance Joel Sokolsky, "Guarding the Continental Coasts; United States Maritime Security and Canada" *Policy Matters* Vol. 6 No. 1 (Montreal: IRPP, March 2005).

[52] Canadian International Development Agency, *CIDA's Social Development Priorities: A Framework for Action* (Ottawa, Minister of Public Works and Government Services Canada, 2000) p. 3.

[53] United Nations, "Millennium Project—Goals and Targets" [http://www.unmil-lenniumproject.org/goals/goals02.htm].

[54] United Nations, *Human Development Report 2005*, (September 2005) Overview p. 2 and 5

[55] Canada. Department of Foreign Affairs, *Canada's International Policy Statement—A Role of Pride and Influence in the World, Development* (2005) p. 3.

[56] Ibid. p. 1.

[57] Ibid. p. 6.

[58] GDP measured in terms of "purchasing power parity" for 2004. See CIA World Fact Book [http://www.cia.gov/cia/publications/factbook/geos/ch.html#Econ]

[59] CIDA, "Statistical Report on Official Development Assistance Fiscal Year 2002–03" (Statistical Analysis Section, CIDA, March 2004) p. 41

[60] CIDA, "Statistical Report on Official Development Assistance Fiscal Year 2002–03" (Statistical Analysis Section, CIDA, March 2004) pp. 28 and 41.

[61] IMF, *Direction of Trade Statistics Yearbook 2004*, (IMF, 2004) p. 237.

[62] CIDA "CIDA Announces New Development Partners: Developing Countries Where Canada Can Make a Difference" (CIDA News Release, April 19, 2005).

[63] CIDA, "Statistical Report on Official Development Assistance Fiscal Year 2002–03" (Statistical Analysis Section, CIDA, March 2004) pp. 28–31.

[64] Louis A. Delvoie, "Canada and International Security Operations: The Search for Policy Rationales" *Canadian Military Journal* (Summer 2000): 13–24.

[65] Canada. Department of Foreign Affairs, *Canada's International Policy Statement—A Role of Pride and Influence in the World, Development* (2005) p. 7.

[66] About $3 billion with the four countries noted. IMF, *Direction of Trade Statistics Yearbook, 2004* (IMF, 2005) p. 119.

[67] Canada. Department of Foreign Affairs, *Canada's International Policy Statement—A Role of Pride and Influence in the World, Development* pp. 3–5.

[68] Jeff Sallot, "Martin Feels EU Heat Over Aid" *Globe and Mail* (June 20,

2005); Senator Colin Kenney, chairman of the Senate's National Security Committee expressed his skepticism at the 0.7 percent goal in July 2005 by noting that if Canadian aid were to be increased to such a level, many states would simply "piss the money away." Cited by Barbara Yaffe, "There's More to the Foreign Aid Equation That Geldof Could Fathom" *The Daily News* (July 11, 2005) p. A6.

[69] Ethiopia's GDP in 2003 was estimated to be about $6.6 billion USD. International Institute of Strategic Studies, *Military Balance 2004-05.*

[70] CIDA, "Statistical Report on Official Development Assistance Fiscal Year 2002–03" (Statistical Analysis Section, CIDA, March 2004) pp. 37 and 41.

[71] International Institute of Strategic Studies, *Military Balance 2004-05.*

[72] IMF, *Direction of Trade Statistics Yearbook, 2004* (IMF, 2005) p. 476.

[73] British aid to Tanzania totalled £110 million in 2005–06 (Source: British High Commission, Tanzania); German aid was nearly 90 million EUR in the 2003 to 2005 period (German Foreign Office); and Dutch aid totalled around 50 million EUR in 2003 and 2004 (Royal Netherlands Embassy, Tanzania).

[74] Based on a total GDP of $6.3 billion USD for Senegal in 2003. International Institute of Strategic Studies, *Military Balance 2004-05.*

[75] Statistics cited in: USAID Budget—Senegal, FY 2002–03 p. 4; found at: [http://pdf.dec.org/pdf_docs/PDACA042.pdf]

[76] As noted in Table Eight, Canadian multilateral and bilateral aid to Senegal totalled just over $28 million, however, the country's bilateral portion was just over $18 million or just under half of United States' level of bilateral assistance.

[77] Figures based on a Guyanese GDP of $777 million USD in 2003. International Institute of Strategic Studies, *Military Balance 2004-05.*

[78] Canadian Council for International Co-operation, "A New Deal for Developing Countries: Strengthening Canadian Aid to Reduce Global Poverty" *Briefing Paper–International Policy Review* (May 2004).

[79] Denis Stairs. "Confusing the Innocent with Numbers and Categories: The International Policy Statement And the Concentration of Development Assistance" (Calgary: CDFAI, December 2005) p.24

[80] David Carment "Effective Defence Policy for Responding to Failed and Failing States" (Canadian Defence and Foreign Affairs Institute, June 2005) p. 11.

[81] Conservative Party of Canada "Stand up for Canada: 2006 Federal Election Platform" pp. 44–45

CHAPTER 6

The Strategies of Three Middle Powers

A *ustralia must have a foreign and trade policy that the Australian community understands and supports. ... Foreign and trade policy [contributes to advancing] Australia's core national interests: the security of the Australian nation and the jobs and standard of living of the Australian people. ...Australia, more than most countries, must pursue an active and tightly focused foreign and trade policy.*

–Australian Foreign Policy White Paper, 1997

Just before 8 a.m. on December 26, 2004, a powerful earthquake struck the Indian Ocean. It generated a massive tsunami that hit the coast of Indonesia within the hour and reached neighbouring countries a few hours later, killing 200,000 or more people in more than 11 countries.[1] Given the scale of the disaster, emergency relief was needed immediately.

Within 36 hours, Royal Australian Air Force C-130s, including many of the brand new "J" model, were delivering essential supplies. A standing Australian disaster plan was activated, disaster and medical teams were dispatched, and a field hospital was operating within days. In a few more days, an Australian amphibious warfare vessel carrying helicopters and landing craft was operating off the coast of Indonesia. Within one week, the Australian aid organization, AUSAID, had committed $1 billion AUS in emergency assistance; a total later increased to $1.8 billion for reconstruction over a five-year period. The response of their government, not ours, was a model.

Australia did not acquire these aircraft, ships, and other assets in order to respond quickly to humanitarian emergencies abroad. Few states do. Rather, the ability to mount such a response results from capabilities the state has acquired to protect important national interests. In Australia's case, focusing both its political and military capabilities on South Asia enabled it to react to the tsunami in a highly effective manner. Australia commits more resources than Canada does to a foreign policy whose ambitions are a great deal less grandiose. It offers a useful case study in how a democratic, western "middle" power can implement an effective and consistent policy with humanitarian side benefits. On a smaller scale, New Zealand and Norway also offer examples of this.

The goals and objectives of these states are somewhat different. Each has adopted a different balance between "realist" and "idealist" dimensions of international policy. The resources they have chosen to allocate to international affairs also differ. But, at different levels, all have been relatively successful in setting clear international policy goals and achieving them.

In general terms, the policy objectives of each of the states considered in this chapter can be ranked in three categories. These are based on the level of influence they believe is necessary to advance their national interests and on the resources they have been prepared to allocate to international affairs. New Zealand is a state with limited or *minimalist* objectives in international affairs; Norway pursues a somewhat broader or *mid-level* international influence, having an activist multilateral policy but only limited leadership aspirations; and Australia is a state that perceives its interests are best served by making a *maximum-level* effort to lead international events in those areas in which the national interest is perceived as most actively engaged.

Each of the states resembles Canada in certain key respects. Although it is much smaller than Canada, New Zealand is a country that has traditionally perceived few direct threats to its own security. New Zealanders have traditionally believed that in a serious conflict, protection by Australia (and the United States Navy) is more or less automatic. Norway's foreign policy is increasingly compared to ours, primarily owing to its activist diplomacy and focus on international development. Like each of the countries considered here, Norway also faces the strategic challenge of protecting a large home territory and large offshore economic zone with a relatively small population.

Lastly, Australia is the country whose strategic situation is most often compared to that of Canada. Both are continent-sized countries with small populations (Australia's is about 60 percent of ours). Both have been relatively free from immediate external threat, though Australia's perception of threats has historically been greater, especially in the 1940s. Both are traditionally classed as "middle powers" with advanced economies (Australia's, again, is about 60 percent the size of ours). The vital difference is that Australia has no overwhelming superpower neighbour. Thus, its regionally focused international policy involves taking a primary leadership role in its immediate neighbourhood.

Like Canada, all the states considered in this chapter have been traditionally aligned with the United States; though, as we shall see, New Zealand's alliance with the United States has now been suspended for 20 years.

Given this range of similarities with Canada, it is instructive to consider the strategic policies of these states: the principal assumptions and foundations that underscore them, the resources that have been committed to them, and the nature of the security discussions that have shaped them.

A *Minimalist* International Policy: New Zealand in World Affairs

New Zealand's international policy is based on a mixture of a hard-nosed realist approach to international security affairs together with considerable idealism in terms of diplomatic policy. On the one hand, the country's security policy is unified and focused on clear national interest-driven priorities. The Defence Policy Framework of 2000 lists these priorities by stating that:

> New Zealand's primary defence interests are protecting New Zealand's territorial sovereignty, meeting shared alliance commitments to Australia and fulfilling obligations and responsibilities in the South Pacific. The wider Asia-Pacific strategic environment, of which we are a part, is also relevant.[2]

New Zealand's aid policy also follows the country's commercial and security interests, and focuses primarily on its immediate neighbourhood. A New Zealand Aid Agency publication notes: "NZAID's core geographical focus is the Pacific region, with which we have close historic and human links."[3] New Zealand spends about the same percentage of its national wealth on both defence and aid as Canada does.[4] However, over 40 percent of New Zealand's $237 million in annual development assistance goes to the states in the South Pacific, and most of the remaining bilateral assistance to Asian nations.[5]

This aid focus is congruent with the country's trade links. Fifty-eight percent of New Zealand's trade is with Asia and Oceania (including Australia–New Zealand's number one trading partner). Naturally, its profile in most states is relatively small. However, as Table 8 shows, there are exceptions in Oceania, where New Zealand's economic footprint is considerably larger than elsewhere in Asia. This provides it with an enhanced role in the so-called micro-states of the South Pacific, particularly in terms of per capita aid.[6]

Table 8: New Zealand Trade and Aid Profile with Selected States in Oceania

	Percentage of That State/ Region's Trade with New Zealand, 2003	New Zealand Aid (Million NZ $ 2003–04)
Solomon Islands	2.7	$13.6
Vanuatu	2.8	$5.7
Papua New Guinea	4.1	$8.5
Fiji	11.6	$2
Samoa	14.8	$7.4
Tonga	34.3	$4.5
Total South Pacific	N/A	$103.5

Source: International Monetary Fund, Direction of Trade Statistics Yearbook, 2004; New Zealand. NZ Aid. "Annual Review 2003–04" pp. 8–9.

However, a policy determination has been made over the past several years that the resources required to achieve New Zealand's principal policy objectives are minimal, particularly on the defence side. In part, this was driven by the fact that during the 1990s, the government did not take the requisite steps to replace obsolescent military equipment. Thus, the new government elected in 1999 reoriented the country's defence policy and declared that: "New Zealand is not directly threatened by any other country and is not likely to be involved in widespread armed conflict."[7]

The military resources that New Zealand has are now focused on territorial security, namely the protection of the country's offshore economic zone (which, at four million square kilometres, is considerable), and peacekeeping in the South Pacific and Southeast Asia. Power projection of combat capabilities is not a priority.

As part of this policy, all jet combat aircraft in the Royal New Zealand Air Force have been eliminated, and the navy is acquiring new offshore patrol vessels with limited combat capability instead of frigates. In the future, both the navy and air force will be largely incapable of major combat operations and, instead, will be almost solely oriented to protecting the national territory against low-level threats. Nevertheless, the army will retain the ability to deploy up to a battalion group (1,000 plus personnel) on international operations for six months and the navy is building a "multi-role ship" (service entry in 2006) to be able to deploy land forces in New Zealand's immediate neighbourhood.

Equipment acquisition is also prioritized for approval by the government in categories that range from projects defined as "beneficial but less critical to achieving policy objectives" all the way to projects described as "necessary to avoid the failure of policy." Thus, the project approval process systematically requires considering possible means in light of identified ends. But even limited defence objectives carry considerable costs and, in 2005, the government approved a program projected to increase defence operating funding gradually but persistently by nearly 50 percent over 10 years.[8]

While New Zealand's security policy is highly focused on achieving clear strategic, political and even economic objectives, the country's diplomatic policy has been more idealistic. In part, this policy orientation flows from the left-of-centre political orientation of the current government. However, the roots of this policy run deep. During much of the Cold War, New Zealand's policy was within the mainstream of Western security policy. It was militarily involved in Korea, Malaya, and Vietnam in the 1950s and 1960s. It also joined two essentially Western alliances:

ANZUS with the U.S. and Australia, and the "five power defence arrangement" with Great Britain, Australia, Singapore, and Malaysia. But with the election of the Labour government of David Lange in 1984, a fundamental reassessment took place.

The new government vigorously embraced the principle of universal nuclear disarmament. Together with several other states, New Zealand has championed both a comprehensive nuclear test-ban treaty and, indeed, the total elimination of all nuclear weapons. And the Lange government passed a law banning all nuclear-powered vessels and any ships potentially armed with nuclear weapons from New Zealand ports and waters.

While New Zealand's diplomatic policy has mostly been declaratory in nature, the ban on nuclear ship visits has been retained. For this New Zealand has paid a diplomatic price. The United States suspended its obligations to defend New Zealand under the ANZUS pact. The alliance has not been restored to date, and no American warships have visited New Zealand for 20 years.

However, there has been a degree of flexibility in New Zealand's foreign policy. It even sent a small military contingent to Iraq after the American invasion despite its opposition to the war. And it did contribute to the war on terror with the occasional symbolic naval presence (one ship) in the Indian Ocean, and through army contingents in Afghanistan.[9] This flexibility has tended to soften the more controversial elements of its policy. Over the longer run, however, the idealist paradigm has had an impact on the way national military capabilities have been perceived by decision-makers. As in Canada, defence spending declined and equipment aged as much through political indifference as through rational strategic decisions.

Overall, one can describe New Zealand's security policy as strategically focused but inward looking, even isolationist, with respect to capabilities. And while the country's broader diplomatic policy has been driven by idealism in key respects tempered by considerable flexibility, the combination of diminishing capabilities and diplomatic idealism has led to growing marginalization and to even more limited international influence. Even so, this has been a price that New Zealand has been willing to pay.

The Political Context for New Zealand's Security Policy

New Zealand's political system is similar to that of Canada, although with respect to international policy-making there are several key differences worth noting that impact on the nature of New Zealand policy. First, New Zealand has placed a much greater emphasis on policy consistency over time, and on the importance of the coordination of objectives among departments. For instance, in New Zealand, the minister of foreign affairs is also responsible for the New Zealand aid agency, for trade policy, and for "Pacific island" affairs. (In Canada, similar responsibilities are divided between three ministers.) The minister also chairs the cabinet committee on external affairs and defence (which also includes the prime minister).

Second, unlike Canada, New Zealand maintains a national intelligence service. Reporting to the prime minister, it has the mandate to "provide the government with timely and accurate intelligence and advice on national security issues."[10] With a focus on Pacific and Asian affairs, such capability affords New Zealand with the expertise necessary to maintain detailed knowledge regarding developments in the region, and to provide the basis for policy actions there.

Third, in contrast to Canada, there is greater potential that the New Zealand parliament will be actively engaged in international policy matters in the future. While minority governments are relatively rare in Canada, they are common in New Zealand. Just over half the members of the 120-seat House of Representatives are elected in single-member constituencies and the rest are elected from party lists based on proportional representation. Since this system was adopted in 1996, no party has obtained an outright majority. While general parliamentary influence over the details of international policy remains limited,[11] any government must rely on the support of other parties to govern. This tends to open up the process of policy formulation and strategic debate to wider debate and broader ideas.

Fourth, as a small power, New Zealand has few pretensions to playing a major global role. This has tended to make the country's international policy more realistic and less driven by inflated self-perception. While the opposition parties have criticized the territorial defence strategy pursued by the Labour Party since 1999, this policy has been sustained through two elections since that time, a factor that seems to lend credence to the idea that a minimalist role in international affairs, and the limited resources that this requires, corresponds with New Zealanders' perceptions of the national interest.

Mid-*Level* International Influence: Norway in World Affairs

Norway's international policy is often compared to that of Canada. Diplomatically, Norway is an active participant in many multilateral forums, and has carved out a kind of niche as an international mediator. It also invests considerable resources in foreign aid. As a Norwegian Foreign Affairs statement notes: "The overarching goal of Norwegian development cooperation is to contribute to lasting improvements in economic, social, and political conditions for the populations of developing countries with special emphasis on ensuring that assistance benefits the poorest people."[12]

At the same time, however, the security dimension of Norway's international policy has a decided national-interest focus. The purpose of Norway's security policy is defined as "safeguard[ing] and promot[ing] national security interests, first and foremost the safety and wellbeing of the Norwegian people."[13] Traditionally, Norway has been willing to devote a high proportion of its national wealth to defence (currently Norwegian defence spending totals some $4 billion USD or 1.9 percent of GDP[14]).

Norway's international policy is based on the maintenance of national independence and on looking after the country's most important national security concerns first, and then on contributing, both through diplomacy and aid policy, to international stability and development. This has served as the essential basis for Norwegian international policy since the Second World War. During World War II, Norway sought safety in neutrality, only to be occupied by the Nazis for five long years. This led to a fundamental policy reassessment after World War II, and Norway became a founding member of NATO in 1949. But Norwegians have jealously guarded their independence and have never joined the European Union,[15] nor permitted the basing of foreign forces on Norwegian territory. Thus, multilateralism has been perceived as an instrument of Norwegian foreign policy, but international organizations have also been kept at a kind of arms length given their potential challenge to Norwegian policy autonomy.

Norwegian defence and security policy reflects this emphasis on national independence. The primary defence objectives are defence of the national territory and of Norway's offshore economic zone. A Norwegian Defence Department statement says:

> In its immediate neighbourhood, Norway must demonstrate that it has the will and the ability to exercise its own sovereignty, as well was being capable of managing national crises and incidents. ... The need to be capable of dealing with the unexpected, especially on or close to our home territory, makes it vital that we have defence forces capable of countering or minimizing such threats.[16]

The emphasis on "the unexpected" requires retention of core capabilities difficult to reconstitute on short notice. These include ground forces capable of defending the national territory, and air and naval forces capable of defending the Norwegian coastline and enormous resource-rich offshore seas that, at two million square kilometres, are six to seven times greater than Norway itself. It also includes a national intelligence service with a primary focus on the requirements of national defence and territorial security.[17]

It is a challenging undertaking for a country with only 4.6 million people. Therefore, for example, the five new frigates and additional small stealth fast-attack craft currently entering service with the navy may be able to contribute to international operations, but their primary purpose is territorial defence. And while the army is planning to make its "ready brigade" more mobile and deployable, its primary mission will remain defence of national territory. In some respects, Norwegian territorial defence priorities mirror those of New Zealand, though Norwegian forces are considerably more robust and highly combat capable.

Norway puts little emphasis on the ability to project significant military power beyond its offshore oceans. No national strategic air or maritime transport is being sought, nor are strategic tanker aircraft; should its F-16 fighters be sent farther afield, Norway is looking to "NATO-wide solutions" on logistical issues. But Norway has been able and willing to use its forces to maintain solidarity with the United States and other allies. Its Special Forces and light infantry served in Afghanistan, and a

Norwegian frigate and small contingents of fighter aircraft are periodically assigned to "show the flag" in allied operations. Steps have also been taken to improve the capabilities of the country's special operations units and, as of January 1, 2005, to establish a battalion-sized rapid reaction unit. Like New Zealand, Norway opposed the decision to go to war in Iraq in 2003. But like New Zealand, it made symbolic contributions to operations there after the invasion, escalating from a few headquarters staff up to 150 people in the first half of 2004.

As already noted, Norway's diplomatic and aid policies are more idealistically driven. This has been the case since the early 1980s when its prime minister, Gro Harlem Bruntland, headed the UN World Commission for the Environment and Development. In the 1990s, it turned to conflict mediation, including central role in the "Oslo Accords" between Israel and the PLO. More recently, it has played similar roles in Sri Lanka and in Guatemala. Especially in the case of Oslo, Norway has sought a kind of diplomatic-niche role in assisting American diplomacy. It is not unlike the role that Canada was able to play in the 1950s, and it is equally dependent on an extremely competent diplomatic service and the right international environment.

But Norway's diplomatic and aid efforts have also been widely dispersed. It is often noted that Norway devotes one of the highest percentages of national wealth to foreign aid. This now totals 0.92 percent of GDP or nearly $2 billion USD, with the goal of achieving 1 percent of GDP in the next few years.

But the dispersal of aid undermines its effectiveness. To some degree, this was recognized in Norway as early as 1989, when a crucial government document submitted to Parliament, sometimes referred to as "the Bible" of Norwegian foreign policy, warned that to have "real influence" Norway must "concentrate her efforts to areas where our interests are considerable or where we have particular experience, traditions, competence or resources."[18] Thus, Norway has identified just seven "partner countries" as the primary recipients of Norwegian aid: Uganda, Mozambique, Malawi, Zambia, Tanzania, Bangladesh and Nepal. This stands in sharp contrast to Canada's 25 development partners.

Nevertheless, the entrenched interests and ideology of the development community have made the focus of efforts a difficult undertaking in practice. Norwegian aid is more broadly dispersed than the seven partner policy might suggest. In 2001, 37 percent of Norway's aid went to countries in Africa, 25 percent to Asia, 12 percent to Eastern Europe, 10 percent to Latin America, and 7 percent to the Middle East.[19] In general, Norway's broader economic profile in many of these states is also limited. All of this suggests that Norway's aid efforts, though exemplary in many respects, fall more into the category of humanitarian rather than development assistance.

Democratic Engagement in the Making of Norway's International Policy

Norway's size and population help keep its government fairly close to its people. As Norwegian defence analyst Olav Riste commented: "The smallness of the country means that there is little distance between the government and the governed, hence the citizen–individually or increasingly through professional organizations–has more influence on national decisions affecting his or her life situation."[20] This also encompasses matters of international policy. A strong strategic culture and a history of national vulnerability make defence a key issue of concern.

Most citizens also tend to be involved in national defence in some capacity. All males face compulsory military service in the armed forces, including reserve force obligations until age 44. In addition, a voluntary "Home Guard" comprised of nearly 80,000 men and women on mobilization, and a civil defence force of about 50,000 when mobilized, are maintained. (Similar organizations in Canada would have about 560,000 and 350,000 people respectively.)

The nature of the political system also provides citizens with a much greater voice in international policy matters. Proportional representation usually ensures that no party has a majority in the Norwegian Parliament. National policies are therefore usually based on compromises between governing and opposition political parties, especially since measures like the ratification of treaties and the surrender of any national sovereignty to a supranational organization require ratification by Parliament. In practice, really major international policy decisions, such as entry into the EU, require approval in a national referendum.

The Norwegian Parliament, or "Storting", has extensive powers over international policy. Its defence and foreign affairs committees not only review planned international expenditures on an annual basis, they actually use their powers to alter and change the budget. In 2001 for instance, the defence committee completely rejected the government's defence proposals, and forced the government to redraft its plans and increase defence spending in the following fiscal year.

The national consensus with respect to Norwegian international policy includes an extensive commitment of resources for both national defence and foreign aid, and an emphasis on quiet diplomacy in support of international security efforts. But while national defence efforts are concentrated and focused on territorial defence and offshore security, Norway's broader diplomacy and aid is more widely dispersed. This decision to disperse resources, coupled with the fact that Norway is a smaller country with limited absolute national resources (its GDP totalled $183 billion USD in 2003), means that the country is essentially a mid-level or niche player in international affairs. The general consensus in Norway is that such a role adequately serves the national interest.

Striving for *Maximum* Influence and Regional Leadership: Australia

Australian international policy is oriented toward achieving one overarching objective: the promotion of the national interest. As discussed in the introduction to this book, the 1997 Australian Foreign Policy White Paper, and other government statements since, have defined Australia's national interests as "advancing the security and prosperity of Australia and Australians." They have differentiated between interests and values with the latter not scorned, but described as creating the framework through which national interests are advocated and advanced rather than being themselves a tool of policy. The *purpose* of Australia's foreign and security policies are interest-based; the *task* is to ensure that these are advanced in keeping with national values.[21]

Australia's specific international policy interests are prioritized on the basis of its interest in different geographic regions. The 2000 Defence White Paper states that:

> Highest priority is accorded to our interests and objectives closest to Australia ... in general, the closer a crisis or problem is to Australia, the greater the likelihood that it would be important

to our security and the greater the likelihood that we would be able to help do something about it.

The same document then outlines five strategic objectives in descending order of importance:

- The defence of Australia and its direct approaches;
- The security of our immediate neighbourhood;
- Stability and cooperation in Southeast Asia;
- Contribute, in appropriate ways, to stability in the wider Asia-Pacific region; and,
- Contribute to efforts of the international community, especially the United Nations, to uphold global security[22]

Weighing means against ends, this 2000 Defence White Paper judged that Australian military power could be very significant in ensuring the stability of countries and territories close to Australia, and that failing to acquire the requisite military capabilities to deal with evolving threats in this region would endanger Australian security.

Thus, Australia spends about 2.7 percent of its GDP on defence (vs. about 1 percent by Canada.)[23] This is funding a major modernization of existing forces. Over the next decade, the navy and air force are also set to acquire new power projection capabilities that include: heavy-lift aircraft; two large helicopter assault ships (due from 2012); three anti-air warfare destroyers with an anti-ballistic missile defence capability (due from 2013); additional troop carrying and combat helicopters (already in service and more to be acquired); new radar surveillance aircraft (due from 2007); the Global Hawk, a long-endurance, unmanned air vehicle (due after 2010); and new strategic tanker aircraft (due from 2007) to support the long-range deployment of air power. The army, in turn, is building up both its light special operations forces and its heavy combat capabilities; the latter by acquiring American-built M1A1 main battle tanks (due from 2007.)

Over the past several years, Australia has taken the lead in major regional military operations, beginning with East Timor in 1999 and the Solomon Islands in 2003. (Further afield, Australian military commitments have been more symbolic, including smaller contingents in Iraq and Afghanistan to support the United States.) Lessons from the East

Timor operation were instrumental in shaping capability objectives originally outlined in the 2000 Defence White Paper; just as the experience of 9/11 and the October 2002 Bali bombings led to further enhancements of military capability objectives in the defence update statement of 2003.

This strategic focus governs the allocation of other resources as well. In 2003, for instance, apart from certain programs in Southeast Africa, Australia's $2.5 billion in annual aid was entirely devoted to Asia (particularly Southeast Asia) and the South Pacific. One of three cornerstones of Australian aid policy is also to ensure that economic benefits flow to Australian companies from the provision of aid. There is little hesitation in integrating (or "tying") aid and commercial policy, which are regarded as mutually reinforcing.[24]

Table 9: Australian Regional Economic and Aid Profile: Trade (Imports and Exports) in 2003 and Aid Levels (2005) with Selected States in Asia and Oceania

	Percentage of Australian Trade with State/Region	Percentage of That State/ Region's Trade with Australia	Australian Development Aid (Millions AUS $)
Solomon Islands	0.024	15.8	$246.8
Papua New Guinea	1	30.4	$492.3
Vietnam	1.1	3.7	$77.3
Thailand	2.4	2.4	$7.0
Malaysia	2.7	2.1	None
Indonesia	2.9	3.7	$301.8
Singapore	3.3	2.5	None
Asia/Oceania Total	58.6	NA	$1,753.6*

Source: International Monetary Fund, Direction of Trade Statistics Year Book, 2004; Australian aid figures from: Australia. Australian Department for International Development "Summary of Australia's Overseas Aid Program 2005–06" *Total comprises Australian bilateral assistance in Asia/Oceania and does not include Australia's global multilateral assistance amounting to $475 million.

As Table 9 shows, Australia's footprint in some small Pacific states is extremely large. The provision of hundreds of millions of dollars in annual assistance to Papua New Guinea and the Solomon Islands allows Canberra to control the development and even the political agenda there.[25] Australian aid to Papua New Guinea comes to nearly $90 per capita, while in the Solomon Islands it amounts to an average of about $458 per person. Even in a country as large as Indonesia, Australia maintains an impressive presence by concentrating its political and economic efforts (its level of aid to that country is 10 times that of Canada.) In response to the tsunami of 2004, Australia was the leading provider of humanitarian assistance to Indonesia.

Although Australia's trade with some of its neighbours–Indonesia, Malaysia, Thailand, Singapore and Vietnam–is relatively small seen from Australia, it is among each of *their* top 10 trading partners. And Australia's share of its trade with the seven countries listed in Table 9 nearly equals the 15 percent it conducts with its own largest partner, Japan. Collectively, Asia and Oceania account for more than 58 percent of Australia's trade. Partly as a result, Australia has emerged as a regional leader in Southeast Asia and the South Pacific. Of course, its political and diplomatic role is reinforced by its defence policy.

Australia's international policy lends its credibility with key allies–notably the United States–and makes Australia a valued partner in regional, and even global, security matters. Historically, Australia has been less reticent than Canada about supporting controversial American political and strategic policies because it understands better the gratitude earned by a friend in need.

While its strategic policy has been interest-driven ("the security and prosperity of Australia and Australians"), humanitarian considerations are not absent. Indeed, one of the pillars of Australian aid policy is to alleviate suffering. And the Australian military has often been at the forefront of assistance delivery after natural disasters in Southeast Asia. But humanitarian concerns have been recognized as distinct from national interests, except in that the ability to respond effectively to humanitarian emergencies in Southeast Asia increases Australia's political influence there. In that sense, humanitarian policy too serves the national interest.

Political Continuity: The Prerequisite for Successful Policy

Australia's international policy of recent years has been characterized by a rather remarkable political consensus. In part, the nature of the policy-making process facilitates such consensus. While the government plays the lead role, parliament has always exercised an important role in oversight and confirmation that also contributes significantly to long-term policy consensus and consistency.

The elected senate is especially important. Its defence committee reviews the government's annual budget and proposed military or aid programs in considerable detail over a number of weeks and months. This not only improves policy in the short run but also acquaints senators, MPs, and political figures in all parties more fully with strategic matters, and the habit and requirements of strategic thinking. This education process in turn produces greater bipartisanship and longer-term policy consensus by limiting the politicization of defence issues. In fact, in the annual 2004–05 defence budget process, the left-of-centre Labor opposition criticized the government for deferring too many projects rather than moving ahead with them promptly.[26]

This reflects the tendency of the opposition Labor party to support the basic strategic realism of the government's assertive international policy. In the lead up to the election of 2004, Labor Defence Critic Chris Evans explained:

> Bipartisan support did emerge over the fundamentals of the government's White Paper, Defence 2000... Labor continues to support the White Paper's priority tasks for the Australian Defence Force ... The tasks signal the common sense of a maritime strategy for Australia, importance of self-reliance, the value of a secure and stable neighbourhood, and a commitment to international operations led by the United Nations and Australia's key allies in the pursuit of broader national strategic objectives. The general consensus does not mean there is complete continuity on all policy and spending issues. Australia has intelligent debate, not thoughtless orthodoxy, and some of Labor's policy priorities have been different from those of the government (for instance, Labor proposed withdrawing Australian troops from Iraq in

2004). Nevertheless, there has generally been agreement on the country's overall strategic direction.[27]

Australia's decision to opt for a coordinated policy approach that emphasizes the national interest is the outcome of a strategic debate that has been underway for some time. After its involvement in Vietnam in the 1960s and 1970s, Australia decided to step back from a forward defence posture to instead emphasize territorial defence. In the 1970s and 1980s, much like Canada, Australia's political engagement overseas tended to emphasize multilateral activities through the United Nations and other international organizations.

But the instability of the post-Cold War period changed that orientation. As one Australian officer writing about this shift in perception has noted, "Australia saw its own 'arc of instability' as requiring more urgent attention, with problems festering in Bougainville, the Solomon Islands, East Timor and beyond, throughout the Indonesian archipelago."[28]

Where ambitions increase, Australian politicians understood, so must capabilities. The previous Labor government began to initiate modest improvements to the armed forces, and then a fundamental restructuring was undertaken by the Liberal-National Party coalition government under Prime Minister John Howard, first elected in 1996.

The process of rethinking strategic policy, while driven by government, was the product of a strategic dialogue that reassessed the nature of the strategic challenges facing the country. It began with the government's Strategic Policy Document of 1997, followed shortly thereafter by the Foreign and Trade Policy White Paper. Only in 2000 was a Defence Policy White Paper produced, outlining the military capabilities required. The result today is that diplomacy, trade, defence, aid, and intelligence capabilities are all pulling in the same direction, focused on advancing the national interest in those regions and countries deemed most important to Australia.

Crucially, this "strategic rethink" has had to involve the Australian Parliament. This flows from a recognition that long-term continuity is essential to success. Parliamentary buy-in and political consensus create the conditions for that consistency over the long term. This engagement is central to ensuring that, in the words of the Foreign Policy White Paper, Australia is able to sustain "a foreign and trade policy that the Australian community understands and supports."[29] The ability to hold that support will be key in determining whether Australia can sustain its current maximalist approach to the conduct of international policy over the coming decade.

Lessons for Canada

The self-perception of many Canadians is that we currently pursue an international policy akin to that of Australia; that we are leaders in world affairs. However, because our policy approach lacks the order and focus of Australia, we simply cannot bring our resources to bear in the same way. While Australia spends a greater percentage of its national wealth on defence, it also spends its wealth better in that it has a long-term plan and clear national priorities. The latter is ultimately more important than spending more money. Indeed, when it comes to foreign aid, Canada spends the same percentage of its national wealth as Australia does, and spends more in absolute dollars. The difference is that Australian resources are concentrated, thus providing a much greater bang for the buck.

Certain assets and capabilities are also entirely missing in Canada. Unlike the other three countries discussed in this chapter, Canada has no national intelligence service. This not only constitutes a missing capability; it also reflects a way of thinking about international affairs that tends to downplay the importance of knowledge-based and realist-driven decision-making.

There are closer parallels between Canadian policy and the policies of New Zealand and Norway. Like New Zealand, we spend about the same percentage of our national wealth on defence and have also been running down our military capabilities, if not quite as steeply. On the diplomatic side, our foreign policy also resembles the idealism of New Zealand's policy approach.

But unlike New Zealand, we are situated next to the United States. Our military free riding and ideologically driven opposition to aspects of American foreign policy therefore has political repercussions that New Zealand's policies do not. New Zealand's free riding has few implications for that country's sovereignty; the same cannot be said for Canada. It is also important to remember that all its idealist rhetoric notwithstanding,

New Zealand pays considerable attention to focusing its limited resources on those issues that matter most to the national interest. This is a lesson that Canada has yet to learn.

For some Canadians, the Norwegian approach to international policy may be a tempting model. Like Canada, Norway has sought to pursue a global diplomatic and aid policy. But this has involved a massive commitment of resources. Norway's aid effort now approaches one percent of its GDP—about four times what Canada is willing to devote. There is little likelihood that Canada will ever spend an equivalent amount. Even if it did, there are fundamental questions as to the effectiveness of widely dispersed development efforts that are unable to capitalize on deeper bilateral economic and trade links.

Nevertheless, some of the successes of Norwegian diplomacy are worth noting. They suggest that Canada would do well to rediscover the benefits of "quiet diplomacy." Rather than focusing primary emphasis on quixotic objectives that are opposed by the great powers, Norway has generally sought to stay in the international policy mainstream. While some, such as Jennifer Welsh, have described Norwegian foreign policy as achieving little more than "fifteen minutes of fame,"[30] there is an important national-interest dimension to such an approach because it builds up credibility where it counts most. Norway's diplomacy has made it a valued diplomatic partner for the United States.

To varying degrees, what is common to all these countries is that effective political institutions are viewed as key to the process of policy making. This led to less inertia and partisanship, and more relevant and rational discussion. It helps develop a strategic culture in which hard questions about appropriate ends and appropriate means are widely discussed. Such a culture, in turn, helps to ensure the long-term policy consistency that is useful to a nation and reassuring to its allies. In Norway and Australia in particular, the national parliaments are more active in overseeing budgets, and in formulating and implementing policy.

It seems clear that to develop and sustain a more effective approach to foreign affairs, Canada must break out of its present "weak state" trap in which politicians produce, and citizens accept, feeble international policy. Chapter seven describes in more detail the nature of the present institutional problem and offers possible solutions.

—NOTES—

[1] Figure cited in United Nations, *Human Development Report 2005*, (September 2005) Overview p. 1

[2] New Zealand, Ministry of Defence "The Government's Defence Policy Framework" (June 2000).

[3] New Zealand. New Zealand Aid "Who is NZAID?" [http://www.Nzaid.govt.nz/about/index]

[4] New Zealand aid spending was actually 0.23 percent of GDP in 2003 vs. 0.24 percent by Canada. New Zealand defence spending was 1.2 percent of GDP vs. 1 percent by Canada. Aid as percentage of GDP as reported by the Organization for Economic Cooperation and Development [OECD – http://www.oecd.org/countrylist/0,2578,en_2649_34485_1783495_1_1_1_1 ,00.html]. Sources for Military spending: International Institute for Strategic Studies, *Military Balance 2004-05*

[5] In total, Pacific nations received $103 million in assistance, Asian nations $35 million, and African states $7 million. The rest of the aid budget was destined for multilateral organizations, New Zealand aid agencies, or emergency relief. New Zealand Aid, "Annual Review 2003–04" pp. 8–9.

[6] In per capita terms, New Zealand's aid efforts in many of these states are also more substantial than they would be elsewhere. New Zealand's aid to the Solomon Islands for instance amounts to about $25 per capita, in Vanuatu $28, and in Samoa and Tonga about $40.

[7] New Zealand, Ministry of Defence "The Government's Defence Policy Framework" (June 2000).

[8] New Zealand. Ministry of Defence. "The Defence Sustainability Initiative: Building a Long-Term Future for the New Zealand Defence Force" (2 May 2005) p. 11. Despite the commitment, consistency in defence policy may be a problem over such a long period. Indeed, just one year earlier (in 2004–05), defence spending was cut by $277 million or 14 percent over the previous year's levels. New Zealand. House of Representatives, "Report of the Foreign Affairs, Defence and Trade Committee, 2004/05 Estimates Vote Defence and Vote Defence Force", p. 3.

[9] New Zealand actually took the lead in 2004 in setting up one of the Provincial Reconstruction Teams in Afghanistan.

[10] The service's "apolitical" function is an integral aspect of the legislation set-

ting up the service. New Zealand. New Zealand Secret Intelligence Service "The NZSIS in Brief" [http://www.nzsis.govt.nz/work/in-brief.html].

[11] Parliamentary input has been limited when it comes to detailed matters such as budgets. For instance, in 2004–05 Parliament's Committee on Foreign Affairs, Defence and Trade devoted fewer than three hours of hearings to the defence budget estimates. New Zealand. House of Representatives, "Report of the Foreign Affairs, Defence and Trade Committee, 2004/05 Estimates Vote Defence and Vote Defence Force", p. 8.

[12] Norway. Ministry of Foreign Affairs, "Focus on Norwegian Development Cooperation—Statement to the Storting on Norwegian Development Cooperation in 2001" p. 24 and p. 39.

[13] Norway. Defence Department, "The Further Modernization of the Norwegian Armed Forces 2005–2008" p. 6.

[14] International Institute for Strategic Studies, *Military Balance 2004-05*

[15] In two referenda, in 1972 and 1994, Norwegian voters rejected EU membership.

[16] Norway. Defence Department, "The Further Modernization of the Norwegian Armed Forces 2005–2008" p. 6.

[17] This defence orientation is reinforced by the fact that the Director-General of Intelligence reports to the commanding General who serves as Norway's "Chief of Defence." See [http://www.mil.no/etjenesten/english/start/article.jhtml?articleID=42381].

[18] Report to Parliament, ("Development Trends in the International Society and Their Effects on Norwegian Foreign Policy") quoted by Olav Riste "Facing the 21 Century [sic]: New and Old Dilemmas in Norwegian Foreign Policy" The Norwegian Atlantic Committee (13/2001).

[19] Ibid p. 65.

[20] Riste "Facing the 21 Century."

[21] See the 2003 update of the 1997 Foreign Policy White Paper. Australia, Department of Foreign Affairs and Trade, *Advancing the National Interest: Australia's Foreign and Trade Policy White Paper* (February 2003).

[22] Australia, Department of Defence, *The White Paper: Defence 2000–Our Future Defence Force.*

[23] GDP measured in terms of purchasing power parity. Source: CIA World Fact Book—Australia: [http://www.cia.gov/cia/publications/factbook/geos/as.html#Econ]

[24] Australia. AusAid. "Australia's Aid Program."

[25] In the Solomons, Australian aid constituted about 25 percent of the GDP, while in Papua New Guinea it was about 10 percent. See International Institute of Strategic Studies, *Military Balance 2004-05;* GDP data at: CIA World Fact Book—Solomons—[http://www.cia.gov/cia/publications/factbook/geos/bp.html; Papua—.../pp.html].

[26] Chris Evans, "Defence Budget—More Money Less Capability" (Labor Party: May 12, 2004). For more detailed discussion of the role of the Australian Parliament in defence policy oversight see: Douglas Bland and Roy Rempel, "A Vigilant Parliament: Building Competence for Effective Parliamentary Oversight of National Defence and the Canadian Armed Forces" *Policy Matters* 5 (Montreal: IRPP, February 2004): 35–42.

[27] Chris Evans, "Iraq: Labor's Perspective", Speech to the Labour Movement Education Association, (Perth: May 21, 2004).

[28] John Blaxland, *Strategic Cousins: Canada, Australia and Their Use of Expeditionary Forces from the Boer War to the War on Terror* (PhD dissertation, Queen's University, 2003) p. 193.

[29] Forward to the Australian Foreign Policy White Paper, 1997 by the Australian Ministers of Foreign Affairs and Trade.

[30] Jennifer Welsh *At Home in the World: Canada's Global Vision for the 21st Century* (Toronto: HarperCollins, 2004) p. 178

CHAPTER 7

Speaking Truth to Power

I f you want to have democratic debate over foreign policy, you have to begin by solving the democratic problem in Canadian politics generally.

–David Frum, author and columnist

In November 1996, Deputy Foreign Minister Gordon Smith and other senior officials were summoned to meet Prime Minister Chrétien to discuss the growing humanitarian crisis in eastern Zaire. However, it did not turn out to be much of a discussion. Mr. Chrétien "had made up his mind when he walked in", Mr. Smith reported, and "there was no holding him back."[1]

The prime minister had decided that Canada would lead this military mission. It was simply too late to ask the important questions: Was the mission realistic? Were the objectives even feasible? There were grave doubts on both points. At the end of the meeting, Deputy Minister of Defence Louise Fréchette and Acting Chief of Defence, Staff Admiral Larry Murray, were said to have left the meeting "shaking their heads and wearing expressions that others read as terror."[2] As noted in chapter three, while the mission did not cost Canadian lives, it was far from being successful.

What is notable about the decision-making that led to the abortive Zaire mission is that the plot line is all too familiar. For example, Prime Minister Trudeau's ill-fated "peace initiative" was launched in 1983, despite warnings from the Department of External Affairs that the whole affair was spurious. That simply led to the department being left out of the policy loop as Trudeau went ahead on his own. But Canada lacked the political clout to undertake such a mission and it was largely ignored by the world community. Yet, as former Trudeau cabinet minister John Roberts recalled, it was simply impossible to say: "No, Prime Minister, you shouldn't undertake a mission to save the world."[3]

Going back somewhat further, limited knowledge and understanding of the international realities in the 1960s led the Diefenbaker government to try to renege on commitments to NATO that it had already made, but not understood, concerning nuclear weapons. The ultimate result for Prime Minister Diefenbaker was the needless collapse of his government. Most governments have made major decisions with inadequate knowledge. Joe Clark's government was forced to backtrack on a promise to move the Canadian embassy in Israel from Tel Aviv to Jerusalem in 1979. The Mulroney and Chrétien governments both made snap decisions in the 1990s to deploy Canadian troops to places like Somalia, Croatia, Bosnia, Kosovo, and elsewhere without really understanding the political and military situation on the ground or the nature of the missions, and without planning possible exit strategies.[4]

Certainly no international policy is perfect. The best planned initiatives can go wrong owing to unforeseen events. The government also has the right to ignore expert advice when making decisions, but it should at least hear the advice before hand. Too often, in Canada, this does not happen, and *ad hoc*, badly informed decision-making becomes characteristic of the way in which international policy decisions are typically made.

A large part of the reason for this is that international policy decision-making in Canada is highly concentrated. More often than not, major decisions are simply made by the prime minister alone, with limited input by others. When the abortive Zaire operation was hurriedly launched by Prime Minister Chrétien in 1996, just four ministers were involved. The decision on the Iraq War in 2003 also involved a very small group of just four ministers (Defence, Finance, Foreign Affairs, and the Solicitor General). It is a decision that really could have gone either way because it was so tied to the personality and prevailing emotions of the prime minister.

In Canada, there are virtually no institutions able to act as an effective check on prime ministerial power in international policy. There is certainly much to debate in Canadian international policy, but little actual debate that matters. This is a problem within both the executive and legislative branches of government. In the present closed system, it is difficult to challenge prevailing orthodoxy or to "speak truth to power." The weakness of national policy-making institutions in Canada is both a result and a cause of our lack of strategic culture. Institutional reform is urgently needed.

Reforming the Executive Branch

It is the nature of the British and Canadian parliamentary system that power over foreign policy is concentrated in a few hands—formerly the monarch and advisory council, now the prime minister and Cabinet. Some have claimed that input to Canadian policy-making is actually fairly diverse. David Last and Glen Milne assert that "important powers and responsibilities are vested in the outer [decision-making] rings", eventually including the media and interest groups.[5] But the appearance of activity is deceptive. Hard questions rarely disturb the councils at the centre of the executive branch.[6] In essence, their decisions are not subject to effective checks and balances or even to thorough *post facto* scrutiny.

Few Canadian politicians are well informed about foreign affairs, and even fewer are in the habit of thinking systematically about international ends that matter and the means needed to achieve them. Since the structure of international policy-making in Canada too often fails to facilitate sound advice, policy ends up based either on a gut reaction by the prime minister that one should "do something" in the face of a major humanitarian or security threat, or on a less noble desire for domestic political gain.

Reactive and *Ad Hoc* Decision-Making

Decision-making in Canadian international policy is often *ad hoc* and reactive. Because Canadian policy has few real priorities, any international event can suddenly become an issue of major concern for the government. If it is a major media issue, as often as not, it becomes a major issue for the Canadian government. *Ad hoc* interdepartmental committees are then quickly formed to assist ministers in addressing the issue.

During the 2003 Iraq War, a temporary committee of "Affected Deputy Ministers"—chaired by a senior civil servant from the Privy Council Office—provided analytical support to the government. But it functioned only from March to September of 2003.[7] The same approach characterized Canada's attempted intervention in Zaire in 1996, the decision to deploy military forces to Afghanistan in 2003, and so on.

These committees usually end up running at full speed simply to keep up. They are assembled to deal with matters that may have never before been regarded as important. They are often inadequate for the task, as they lack the hard expertise required to support a major initiative in a policy area heretofore unfamiliar. Gordon Smith recalls that during the Zaire mission:

> I found that even within Foreign Affairs, we were right at the breaking point. I simply dropped everything else I was doing as deputy minister and handled this one file. It was all we could do to cope. And I'm not sure there was an adequate appreciation of just what was involved for both the defence department, militarily, and Foreign Affairs, diplomatically, at bringing together this whole operation.[8]

Formally, decision-making in Canada is concentrated in Cabinet and sub-cabinet committees with broad and often vague mandates.[9] But these are by-passed or ignored whenever the prime minister chooses to do so. Under Jean Chrétien, there were no Cabinet committees specifically focused on international policy at all. Instead, such matters were dealt with by Chrétien himself and any ministers he chose to involve on an *ad hoc* basis or, bizarrely, by the Cabinet Committee for the Social Union. Two analysts recently concluded that the formal Cabinet structure actually provides very little insight into how decisions are made in Canada and that "without knowledge of personalities, knowledge of structures and committee names is almost meaningless."[10]

Even the setting of broader policy directions for the government involves *ad hoc* committees and scattered political attention. The government's response to 9/11 was to form an "*Ad Hoc* Committee of Ministers on Public Security and Anti-Terrorism." Similarly, Prime Minister Chrétien generally only attended one meeting a year on intelligence and security matters to set "policy priorities."[11]

Officially, the Martin government identified this as a problem upon taking office and made a number of changes. For the first time in at least a decade, a Cabinet committee on global affairs was established, chaired by the minister for Foreign Affairs. (A committee on Foreign Affairs and National Security was continued in the Harper government, but neither Martin nor Harper were members of those committees). In 2005, the International Policy Statement (IPS) announced the creation of a "Stabilization and Reconstruction Task Force"; its task is to improve the government's ability to respond to crises as they arise.[12]

Yet, despite these reforms, there is no evidence that there was any recognition of the need to bring greater focus and cohesion to international policy *in advance* of particular crises, to sort what is important from that which is either discretionary or irrelevant. This is because there has been limited understanding of the fact that policy decisions need to be better informed and grounded in a clear understanding of the national interest. Paul Martin's highly personal decision to backtrack on his initial support for ballistic missile defence in 2005 was more reactive, ill-considered, and damaging to Canada than any decision taken during the Chrétien years. This suggests that the decision-making process remained as cumbersome and politicized as ever;[13] that in Canada, as one important American commentator put it, "politics trumps security."[14]

The Problem of Policy Coordination

Central prime ministerial direction in foreign policy tends to be limited to issues of major interest to the national media and which, therefore, are highly political. (Obvious examples include Jean Chrétien taking personal charge of the Iraq War file and the 1996 Zaire mission.) The result is that international policy in most other areas tends to be uncoordinated and driven by inertia. The Auditor General of Canada has listed as many as 17 different departments and agencies that may be engaged in issues of national security alone.[15] In one way or another, most federal departments may at times have some interest in some aspect of international policy.

As discussed in chapter five, coordination among only the three principal international policy departments is difficult enough. More often than not, they tend to pursue their own politically and bureaucratically driven objectives, sometimes in conflict with one another. David Dewitt of York University notes that the "human security" agenda of former foreign minister Lloyd Axworthy was never really accepted by the Department of National Defence.[16] David King, of the U.S. National Defence University, has commented on how the 1994 Defence Policy and 1995 Foreign Policy White Papers "read as if they could be from different countries."[17] Meanwhile, the distinctive culture and world-view of the

Department of National Defence in comparison to CIDA was dramatically illustrated in comments in the *Canadian Army Journal* by Lt. Colonel Pat Stogran, who commanded the army's battle group in Afghanistan in 2002. "The time is long overdue ... for agencies such as CIDA, to pull their head out of the clouds and face realities," such as the need to cooperate with military forces on foreign missions.[18]

The International Policy Statement continued to reflect the different priorities of the key departments. For example, while the Commerce Paper was rigidly focused on economic interests with no reference to human rights in trade policy, the Development and Diplomacy Papers were permeated with references to the central importance of human rights advocacy in building a stable world order.[19]

When more consistent policy coordination actually occurs in Canada, it has been more fortuitous than planned. When Canada initiated its mission in Afghanistan in 2003 and attempted to integrate the diplomatic, development, and military dimensions of policy in the operation, the relationship between the three relevant ministers—Foreign Affairs, CIDA, and Defence—proved critical. But, as one Foreign Service officer reported, this was largely because the three ministers just happened to get along and decided to meet regularly to good effect. That was their choice. Had they not done so, there were no permanent inter-departmental coordination mechanisms to facilitate that vital cooperation.[20] Other than the creation of the Stabilization and Reconstruction Task Force to deal specifically with international crises, the IPS did not contain any measures to make such cooperation, both at the ministerial and bureaucratic levels, systematic across Canada's international policy.

If Canada is to develop a more serious and effective approach to international policy, the decision-making process must be reformed and better coordinated. The attention devoted by political leaders to international affairs must become systematic and well informed. This is particularly imperative because, in the Canadian political system, ministers frequently bring even less advanced knowledge to their portfolios than in other democracies. Given the singularly rapid turnover among, and partisan quality of, appointments to government departments, non-partisan expert advice is especially desirable.

The Absence of Subject Area Expertise

In a country in which politics often trumps security, it is not surprising that the provision of non-political analysis to the prime minister and Cabinet is weak. Such analytical ability flows from an understanding of the realities of the international system. It is the product of subject-specific expertise that results from the study of history, geography, politics, and language in international relations. In the Canadian government, however, subject-specific expertise is not generally held in high regard.

As discussed in chapter five, Foreign Affairs Canada (FAC) recruits its foreign service officers as policy generalists. These individuals do not necessarily have professional qualifications in a particular foreign policy area prior to entering the department. Even if they have expertise in particular subject area in international affairs, they might not work in that subject area throughout their entire careers. Postings within Foreign Affairs are generally only about three years in duration. Thereafter, officers are usually reassigned to a different country or policy area. This makes it somewhat difficult to develop real expertise in one particular subject area, including languages, while working in the department. Just when knowledge begins to accumulate, a person is generally moved to the next assignment.

Officials of the Privy Council Office (PCO), whose "global affairs" and "Canada-U.S." secretariats provide policy advice to the prime minister and Cabinet on international policy issues, are also often policy generalists. Headed by a senior foreign policy advisor, these secretariats provide briefing materials for the prime minister and Cabinet, drawing on information provided by line departments.[21] However, such advice is generally not politically neutral and, instead, is careful to reflect government policy and prime ministerial priorities. Therefore, it may or may not reflect the realities of the international system.

Since the absence of a national security and international relations focus in the PCO was criticized in the past, Prime Minister Martin initiated some well-publicized changes. These sought to elevate the importance of national security matters in Cabinet deliberations. Mr. Martin appointed a "national security advisor" soon after taking office, and created an "Advisory Council on National Security" that drew on individuals from the private sector. But neither deals specifically with international policy. Indeed, the Advisory Council meets only two to four times a year, has no decision-making authority, and no role with respect to the implementation of the advice it may provide.[22]

The national security advisor, in turn, heads two intelligence secretariats within the PCO, which provide intelligence-related advice to the prime minister and Cabinet. But this role, too, only extends to international policy indirectly. The national security advisor himself may not have any professional background in international affairs. For instance, in April 2005, William J.S. Elliott was appointed as national security advisor. Trained as a lawyer, Mr. Elliott has served in departments such as Transport Canada and Indian Affairs. While, since 1998, he acquired background in security-related activities in the PCO, Fisheries and Oceans, and Transport Canada, he did not appear to have a professional background in international affairs.[23]

International policy analysts with subject-specific expertise are few and far between. One division within the Department of National Defence, the Directorate of Strategic Analysis (D Strat A), does provide expert non-partisan analysis. Its staff members are hired specifically for their professional qualifications in particular subject areas of international relations. However, "D Strat A" is only a small director-level think tank buried within the policy group of DND. It numbers only about half a dozen professional staff. Its policy influence, even within DND, is limited. In general, it is kept far distant from the centre of government, where the most important policy decisions are made.

The absence of independent bodies in Canada that can provide non-political analysis directly to the prime minister and Cabinet stands in marked contrast to other countries, such as Australia. In Australia, as in Canada, Cabinet committees are formed at the discretion of the prime minister. The most important committee for international affairs in Australia is the National Security Committee. This committee's mandate is to engage in "strategic policy development" and address all major issues of medium- and long-term relevance to Australia's national security.[24]

The National Security Committee is supported by an Office of National Assessments (ONA). Reporting directly to the prime minister, the ONA produces analytical assessments of international developments. It assists the prime minister, ministers, and departments in the formation of policy and plans. Crucially, it is "not subject to external direction on the content of its assessments, and is independent of any department or authority."[24] ONA analysts "are specialists in their field, which could be political or economic studies of a particular country or region, transnational economic issues, or a strategic discipline, e.g., nuclear weapons proliferation."[25] This office, in conjunction with other departments and agencies such as the Australian Secret Intelligence Service, facilitates the provision of non-political and subject-specific analysis to the prime minister and Cabinet on international relations issues that face the country.

Any state that seeks to play a relevant role in international affairs must act on the basis of informed analysis. Certainly, any state that purports to have as ambitious an agenda as "nation-building" urgently requires subject-specific expertise. If Canadian international policy objectives are to have credibility, the current gap in policy expertise must be addressed.

Central Agency Reform and "Speaking Truth to Power"

To facilitate interest-based policy planning and better coordination, an effective central agency is required. Such a body would be staffed by a range of professionally trained experts, and would provide analysis and advice *upstream* to policy-makers on a permanent basis. Like the ONA in Australia, it would have the mandate to "speak truth to power" by providing non-partisan, interest-driven analysis. Simultaneously, it would also have a useful *downstream* role by better coordinating the policies of all international departments and agencies. An additional step that is long overdue is that such an agency should be complemented by a Canadian intelligence service, which would provide a national perspective of international security challenges facing the country.

Two options exist for creating a new central policy agency. The first option is to establish an analytical agency, similar to the ONA, along with a policy secretariat in the PCO that would have the complementary task of policy coordination.[26] The second option is more formal: to create a statutory "Canadian Security Council" akin to the National Security Council (NSC) in the United States. The mandate of the NSC is described on its Web site:

> The National Security Council is the President's principal forum for considering national security and foreign policy matters with his senior national security advisors and cabinet officials. ... The Council also serves as the President's principal arm for coordinating these policies among various government agencies.[27]

There are precedents for creating a statutory central agency with a widespread information and coordination mandate in Canada. The Federal Treasury Board is a statutory committee of the Privy Council with specific legal responsibilities with respect to national finances, staffed by financial and budgetary experts. A Canadian Security Council is most unlikely to become as powerful as the Treasury Board, but it could certainly become useful in the same kind of way, especially if given a legal foundation that makes it difficult to circumvent.

Whatever option is chosen, it is important that any new structure should take what Douglas Bland of Queen's University has called a "'Canadian perspective." This means that such a mechanism "should not be composed of 'representatives' sent by departments to ensure that the home team is protected from centralist decisions. Rather the mechanism should be especially designed to build coherence between intentions and outcomes."[28]

Some have objected to creating such a mechanism in Canada. Laval University professor Albert Legault submitted a report to Prime Minister Chrétien in 1997, questioning whether Canada's foreign policy was important enough abroad or among voters and politicians here at home to warrant such an organization. He also warned that such an organization might be as readily by-passed as today's more *ad hoc* structures, and that it would increase rather than reduce bureaucratic infighting, especially between itself and Foreign Affairs. He also felt that it could make decision-making even less transparent than it is today and further shift responsibility away from line ministers to the Prime Minister's Office.[29]

Some of these arguments are not convincing. First, if foreign policy is not important to Canadian voters or leaders, they are then in more urgent need of informed advice on a subject they tend to ignore. Second, power in international affairs is already concentrated in the hands of the prime minister. It is difficult to imagine it being any more concentrated as a result of such a reform. If anything, international policy would become more reflective of a genuine national interest rather than being the private preserve of the prime minister, as it often is at present.

Third, as noted earlier, it is certainly the government's prerogative to ignore analysis and advice that it does not like, but it should at least be made aware of the advice. This can only make for a more realistic and better international policy. Fourth, as for the danger of greater infighting within the bureaucracy, we should get away from the notion that debate and discussion are negative. Canada's leadership suffers from too few perspectives on key foreign matters, not too many.

It is important that the government should recognize that Canada's international policy cannot be effective in the absence of better coordination, subject-specific expertise, and, above all, interest-based policy planning. A mechanism that is able to transform the way in which international policy is made in Canada will constitute the first step toward a more serious international policy, reflective of both strategic realities and the national interest.

The Need for a Vigilant Parliament

As we have seen, parliamentary engagement plays a key role in the international polices of both Australia and Norway, while in New Zealand it is less central.

Parliamentary engagement is important in international policy-making for several reasons. Engagement in Parliament builds the knowledge base of MPs who might one day become Cabinet ministers with international policy responsibilities. Parliament should provide oversight of international policy matters by holding government accountable for its actions. And it is Parliament that should determine how the money of taxpayers is spent on matters of international policy.

Most importantly, it is only in Parliament that there is the basis for consensus and policy legitimacy through an inclusive debate and discussion between elected representatives from all political parties and all regions of the country. In other words, Parliament is crucial for building a viable strategic culture. Former U.S. deputy defense secretary John Hamre described the purpose of congressional oversight as "building a national basis for your program; you're building that national support."[30]

It is notable that the Commission of Inquiry that looked into the many problems in the military mission in Somalia concluded that:

> The quintessential condition of control of military and all aspects of national defence is a vigilant Parliament. ... Parliament must exercise greater diligence in critically monitoring the terms agreed to or set by the government for the employment of Canadian Forces overseas and safeguarding members of the

Armed Forces from unreasonable risks; it must also monitor the operations of commanders and troops in the field.[31]

But in Canada, Parliament is a very weak institution. Generally, Parliament has very little real control over budgetary matters. (Even in a minority government, the budgetary influence of opposition parties is limited to a few higher profile issues; in a majority government that influence fades to zero.) Parliament has few real tools at its disposal to ensure that the government is held to account for its actions. Committees that should exercise real oversight usually do not matter. The daily ritual of Question Period is a melodramatic and mostly farcical affair, while debates are largely irrelevant to shaping the policy of the day.[32]

The contrast between Canada and most other democracies is striking. In Norway, the national Parliament has real power over budgetary issues. Committees matter. In Australia, an elected senate scrutinizes the annual spending proposals of the government in great detail.[33] The committees in Canada's Senate do provide good advice, but the Senate is unelected, has little power, and no democratic legitimacy.

These factors all serve to strengthen the already considerable control that the executive exercises in the realm of international policy.

Clearly, comprehensive reform is necessary to make Parliament relevant, effective, and engaged in building a national strategic culture. Leaving aside the major issues that require urgent attention, such as democratizing the Senate, there are measures that could be taken to make the House of Commons more relevant. In relation to international policy, the most important of these is the empowerment of the House committees. Placing MPs on committees for the life of Parliament, without the ability to remove them for anything but wrongdoing, would be a crucial step in enhancing the independence of committees and reducing the control that party leaders currently exercise over them. Going further and allowing MPs, on the basis of their parliamentary seniority, to choose the committees on which they wish to serve would further enhance a culture of independence among MPs.

Changing the culture in Parliament is central to making it effective. Only in a culture in which the independence of MPs is the norm will committees exercise a more effective role on budgetary and policy matters. The Constitution of Canada already gives committees significant theoretical power, including the discretion to reduce or eliminate particular expenditures. It is the culture of tight discipline and government control that ensures that this almost never occurs, leaving the prime minister and cabinet unfettered control over all aspects of international policy.[34]

Democratic debate and discussion must serve as the basis for a more serious Canadian strategic culture in which the national interest serves as the basis for policy. In this respect, David Frum has stated: "If you want to have democratic debate over foreign policy, you have to begin by solving the democratic problem in Canadian politics generally."[35]

We now turn to a discussion of Canada's national interests.

—NOTES—

[1] John Hay, *Conditions of Influence: A Canadian Case Study in the Diplomacy of Intervention*, Occasional Paper No. 19 (Ottawa Norman Patterson School of International Affairs) p. 9.

[2] Ibid. p. 9.

[3] J.L. Granatstein and Robert Bothwell, *Pirouette: Pierre Trudeau and Canadian Foreign Policy* (Toronto: University of Toronto Press, 1990) p. 366.

[4] See discussion in Roy Rempel, *The Chatter Box: An Insider's Account of the Irrelevance of Parliament in the Making of Canadian Foreign and Defence Policy* (Toronto: Breakout Educational Network/Dundurn Press, 2002)

[5] David Last and Glen Milne "National Security Decision-Making" in David Last and Bernd Horn ed. *Choice of Force: Special Operations for Canada* (Kingston: School of Policy Studies, Queen's University, 2005) p. 136.

[6] See for instance Donald Savoie, *Governing from the Centre: The Concentration of Power in Canadian Politics* (Toronto: University of Toronto Press, 1999).

[7] David Last and Glen Milne "National Security Decision-Making" in David Last and Bernd Horn ed. *Choice of Force: Special Operations for Canada* p. 139.

[8] underground royal commission, Documentary *Question of Honour*, Episode Four "The Bungle in the Jungle."

[9] See Rand Dyck, *Canadian Politics: Critical Approaches* (Toronto: Nelson, 2004) p. 517. See also: Glen Milne, *Making Policy: A Guide to the Federal Government's Policy Process* (Ottawa: Glen Milne Publishing 2004) pp. 48–49.

[10] David Last and Glen Milne "National Security Decision-Making" in David Last and Bernd Horn ed. *Choice of Force: Special Operations for Canada* p. 143.

[11] Senate. Standing Committee on National Security and Defence, *Canadian Security and Military Preparedness*, (February 2002) p. 61.

[12] Canada. *Canada's International Policy Statement Overview Paper* (2005) p. 14.

[13] See Derek Burney's critique of the new management structure in: D.H. Burney "Canada-US Relations: Promise Pending?" *In the Canadian Interest? Assessing Canada's International Policy Statement* (Canadian Defence and Foreign Affairs Institute, November 2005) p. 13

[14] This is certainly appears to be the perception in Washington. See discussion in David T. Jones "When Politics Trumps Security: A Washington Vantage Point" *Policy Options* (IRPP: May 2005): 45–50

[15] Auditor General of Canada, *Report of the Auditor General of Canada to the House of Commons, Chapter 3: National Security in Canada–The 2001 Anti-Terrorism Initiative* (March 2004) pp. 5–7.

[16] David Dewitt "National Defence vs. Foreign Affairs" *International Journal* LIX (Summer 2004): 579–595.

[17] David L. King "We Need a Romanow Commission for Defence and Foreign Policy" *Policy Options* (April 2002): 10.

[18] Lt. Colonel Pat Stogran, "Fledgling Swans Take Flight: The Third Battalion, Princess Patricia's Canadian Light Infantry in Afghanistan" *Canadian Army Journal* 7,3 / 7,4 (Fall/Winter 2004): 18.

[19] For example, while the Diplomacy Paper notes the general and theoretical importance of human rights issues in Canadian international policy, the Commerce Paper makes no reference to human rights issues at all when discussing the specifics of Canadian-Chinese trade relations. *International Policy Statement* (2005) Diplomacy Paper, pp. 15–17 and 24–25; Commerce Paper p. 16.

[20] Interview with Foreign Service Officer, June 2004.

[21] For more information see: Glen Milne, *Making Policy: A Guide To the Federal Government's Policy Process* pp. 8, 15 and 40

[22] See advisory council on national security "terms of reference" at: [http://www.pco-bcp.gc.ca/default.asp?Language=E&Page=PCOsSecretariats&sub=si&doc=tor_e.htm]

[23] Prime Minister's Office. "Prime Minister Announces the Appointment of His National Security Advisor" *News Release* (April 7, 2005)

[24] In this capacity, it met 36 times in 2002-03. Australia. Department of the Prime Minister and Cabinet, "Output 3.1 International Policy" [pmc.gov.au/annual_reports/2002-03/performance/outpus3_1.htm]

[25] See Australia, Office of National Assessments: [http://www.ona.gov.au/index.shtml]

[26] See for instance, Jane Boulden *A National Security Council for Canada?* (Kingston: Queen's School of Policy Studies Claxton Paper No. 2, 2000) pp. 32–34.

[27] United States. National Security Council "National Security Council Function" at: whitehouse.gov/nsc/.

[28] Douglas Bland, "Canada and Military Coalitions: Where, How and with Whom?" in Hugh Segal ed. *Geopolitical Integrity* (Montreal: IRPP, 2005) p. 140.

[29] Albert Legault, "Bringing the Canadian Armed Forces into the Twenty-First Century" (Department of National Defence, Report to the Prime Minister, 1997) Part I–Civilian and Military Powers.

[30] John Hamre, interviewed by Robert Roy of Stornoway Productions, September 2001.

[31] Canada. Somalia Commission of Inquiry, *Dishonoured Legacy: The Lessons of the Somalia Affair*, Executive Summary (Ottawa: Minister of Public Works and Government Services Canada, 1997) p. ES-46. Report of the Commission of Inquiry into the deployment of Canadian Forces to Somalia.

[32] For a discussion, see: Rempel, *The Chatter Box* ch 2–4 and Douglas Bland and Roy Rempel, *A Vigilant Parliament: Building Effective Parliamentary Oversight of National Defence and the Canadian Armed Forces* (Montreal: IRPP Policy Matters Series, Vol. 5 No. 1 February 2004) pp. 25–28.

[33] In Norway, for example, where committees play a pivotal role in the annual budgetary process, parliamentary staff may potentially be supported by up to 440 staff serving the Norwegian Auditors office. See discussion in Douglas Bland and Roy Rempel, *A Vigilant Parliament: Building Effective Parliamentary Oversight of National Defence and the Canadian Armed Forces* pp. 37–39 and 44

[34] For a more in-depth discussion of committee reform ideas see: Douglas Bland and Roy Rempel, *A Vigilant Parliament: Building Effective Parliamentary Oversight of National Defence and the Canadian Armed Forces*

[35] underground royal commission interview with David Frum, March 27, 2004.

CHAPTER 8

Canada's National Interests

T *he only real imperative in Canadian foreign policy is Canada's relationship with the U.S.*

–Denis Stairs, et al, *In the National Interest*, 2003*

In the opening sentence to his 2005 book, *The Polite Revolution*, columnist John Ibbitson claimed that: "Not too long ago, while no one was watching, Canada became the world's most successful country."[1] The claim is certainly audacious. In some respects, Canada is indeed quite successful. But as we have seen in this book, in terms of international policy, such a statement is far from reflective of contemporary reality.

That Canada is a great place to live for most Canadians is not in doubt. Rich in natural resources, its people are prosperous and enjoy a high standard of living. Canada consistently ranks among the 20 richest countries in the world in terms of per capita GDP and per capita purchasing power parity. Its people are among the healthiest in the world, with the average life expectancy of Canadians now close to 80 years. Canada is a vast country of almost limitless opportunity for its 32 million inhabitants.

But what are the sources of our "success" or prosperity? How solid are the foundations of that prosperity? Are our national leaders fully aware of just how dependent Canadian prosperity is on our neighbour to the south?

To his credit, Mr. Ibbitson correctly points out that our relationship with the United States is the anchor of our prosperity. Not only is it the anchor of our prosperity, there are absolutely no alternatives to the

---

* The other authors of *In the National Interest* are: David J. Bercuson, Mark Entwistle, J.L. Granatstein, Kim Richard Nossal and Gordon S. Smith.

Canada-U.S. relationship. There are no alternatives in a political sense. There are no alternatives in a strategic sense. And there are certainly no alternatives in an economic sense.

While in the back of their minds Canadians may know this to be true, for some reason we often pretend otherwise. For example, when the United States initially announced in 2005 that it would ignore rulings of NAFTA tribunals in the ongoing softwood dispute, several Canadian politicians argued that Canada should instead seek closer trade relations with countries such as China and India; even that NAFTA might be reviewed.[2]

But this is unrealistic. As illustrated in Table 10, Canada's total trade with China and India combined is no more than 3.4 percent of our total world trade. In contrast, our total trade with the United States stands at 75 percent. Canadian trade with California alone is nearly twice as much as that with China and India combined. It is most unlikely that trade with China, India, or any other combination of states will ever grow in such a way to significantly change such percentages. The Canadian economy is largely carried by its trading relationship with the United States. Canada's trade surplus (more exports than imports) with the United States compensates for the trade deficit that Canada has with almost every other country in the world, including China, India and every other major trading partner (other than Belgium in 2003). For most other countries, Canada is barely a blip on their economic radar screen.[3] Despite setbacks like the softwood and beef disputes, our economic relationship with the United States will always be the anchor of our prosperity and way of life.

What should seriously concern Canadians when the United States ignores the rulings of NAFTA trade tribunals is that this is illustrative of the dangers of what being treated as a protectorate is like. Under such a relationship the rules are simply dictated to Canada rather than being settled through mechanisms that are characteristic of a genuine partnership.

Given this reality, building and maintaining a healthy, cooperative partnership relationship with the United States ought to be the central priority of Canadian international policy.

Table 10: Canada's Top 21 Trading Partners, 2003

Rank	State	Imports from State (millions USD)	Canadian Exports to State (millions USD)	Total trade with State (millions USD)	Percentage of Canadian Trade with State	Approxim-ate num-bers of Canadian Diplomats in State*
1	USA	$132,928	$235,241	$368,169	75	136
2	China	$12,201	$3,215	$15,416	3.1	59
3	Japan	$8,972	$5,610	$14,582	3	42
4	UK	$5,948	$3,812	$9,760	2	42
5	Mexico	$7,959	$1,546	$9,505	1.9	27
6	Germany	$5,659	$1,930	$7,589	1.5	30
7	France	$3,251	$1,525	$4,776	1	44
8	S. Korea	$3,360	$1,312	$4,672	0.95	17
9	Italy	$2,955	$1,195	$4,150	0.85	18
10	Norway	$2,825	$650	$3,475	0.71	4
11	Taiwan	$2,467	$847	$3,314	0.68	13
12	Netherlands	$1,105	$1,099	$2,204	0.45	13
13	Australia	$1,051	$943	$1,994	0.41	14
14	Brazil	$1,311	$611	$1,922	0.39	23
15	Belgium	$761	$1,117	$1,878	0.38	14
16	Malaysia	$1,497	$342	$1,839	0.37	11
17	Algeria	$1,571	$253	$1,824	0.37	6
18	Ireland	$1,242	$344	$1,586	0.32	4
19	Thailand	$1,227	$312	$1,539	0.31	15
20	Sweden	$1,331	$200	$1,531	0.31	4
21	India	$931	$504	$1,435	0.29	46

* Refers to Foreign Affairs diplomats and other departmental employees at the embassy and in consulates around the country. Source: International Monetary Fund, *Direction of Trade Statistics Yearbook, 2004* and Foreign Affairs Canada. Access to Information Request No. A-2004-00285/ac.

What Is the National Interest?

The fundamental national interest of the government of Canada is to protect and promote the well being of Canadians. To that end, the government is therefore responsible for forging an international policy that will create the conditions and the environment in which this is possible.

However, as we have seen, the Canadian government has not done a very good job in this regard. The very term "national interest" is one that has been used in Canadian international policy relatively infrequently or in a relatively cursory fashion. This is a large part of the current problem.

The International Policy Statement (IPS) of 2005, for instance, noted that Canada has three "fundamental interests"—prosperity, security, and responsibility.[4] Yet beyond noting them once within a 120-page set of documents, there is little exploration of what these terms require and mean practically. Prosperity and security are indeed the core goals of any state's international policy, but they are very broad concepts that require focus, trade-offs, and specific policy objectives and priorities. The IPS provided little sense as to what these might be.

The elevation of responsibility to the status of a fundamental Canadian interest also expands the notion of national interest considerably. The term "national interest" is often referred to by the French term *raison d'etat* and constitutes a state's "goals and ambitions whether economic, military, or cultural."[5] In liberal democracies, interests are national objectives related to the collective prosperity and security of the people.

In that context, it is difficult to conceive of responsibility as an interest. The IPS sought to justify the notion that responsibility is a fundamental Canadian interest by arguing that:

> Canada is a vibrant liberal democracy, with both regional and global responsibilities, whose success is intimately tied to a stable international order.

> Effective multilateral governance is essential for Canadian security and prosperity. Multilateral action is in turn dependent on states accepting their responsibility to both their citizens and to other countries.[6]

Responsibility defined in this way elevates multilateralism to a predominant position in the hierarchy of Canadian international policy concerns. Canada's international policy seeks to promote *both* the objectives of the Canadian people and remain responsible to other countries (whether democratic or undemocratic) as well as to international organizations. In effect, multilateral engagement becomes an end in itself; the moral equivalent of the government's responsibility to the Canadian people.

The notion is based on a false assumption. Multilateral governance is described as "essential for Canadian security and prosperity", in effect a kind of precondition for the country's security and prosperity. But this is incorrect. As a North American power, Canada is effectively shielded from many of the most serious ill effects of international instability. A really effective Canada-U.S. relationship is the only thing *necessary* for Canadian prosperity and security.

As noted in the introduction to this book, a large part of the problem is that Canadians consistently confuse interests and values. John Ibbitson claims that "interests *are* values" [emphasis in the original].[7] Michael Ignatieff argues that Canada should be a global champion of "peace, order and good government" as reflective of both Canada's national interests and national values.[8] Two leading academic writers in this subject area, Don Macnamara and Ann Fitz-Gerald, also discuss values and interests interchangeably. They contend that Canadian "national interests—values and goals—can be derived from existing policy and constitutional documents." "The core values", they assert, "are the values we expect our troops to defend and, if necessary, die for."[9]

But since values are engaged everywhere, they cannot serve as the basis for a credible and effective international policy. It is far from clear, for example, that Canadians are willing to see their troops fight and die in large numbers for the values articulated in the Constitution or the Charter of Rights if the crisis in which they are engaged has no real relevance for Canadian security or prosperity. (And it is simply wrong to argue, as has been the case in recent years, that any security challenge anywhere in the world poses a direct danger to Canada.[10])

If Canadian international policy is to be credible and effective, then policy objectives must be tightly focused on protecting and promoting the real economic, political, and security interests of the Canadian people. This means setting national priorities, not on the basis of rather amorphous moral statements, or on the issues that happen to prevail in the news from day to day, or even on the basis of the personal feelings of the prime minister, but rather on the basis of a careful assessment of what will most benefit the country and its citizens.

It is in how these goals are implemented that values come into play. The national values of any liberal democracy will dictate that the implementation of national interest objectives cannot be based on a ruthless "beggar thy neighbour" approach. Instead, they should be consistent with some of the themes referred to in Canadian foreign policy documents, such as democracy and the rule of law, the dignity of the human person, sustainable economic well-being, and so on. In other words, while *interests should serve as the essential goals and objectives of state policy, values are the lenses through which policy makers view the choices with which they are confronted in relation to those interests.*

Canadian National Interests: From the General to the Specific

The process of translating the general interests that Canada has in prosperity and security into specific policy objectives and priorities must begin with a rational assessment of Canada's geo-strategic position. As early as 1962, the Canadian strategist R. J. Sutherland spoke of certain "invariants" in Canadian strategy. These, he postulated, were most important in determining the agenda of Canadian international policy. He wrote that these invariants revealed: "important areas where there is no choice, however much we as Canadians might like to believe that there is."[11]

Sutherland argued that the most important invariant is geography, the most important consequence of which binds Canada and the United States firmly together. It was also evident to Sutherland that geography and the nature of the North American economy made Canada and the United States "a single target system" for any potential adversary.[12] Ten years later, in 1972, the British strategist Colin Gray referred to a similar political and economic imperative. Although liberal Canadian nationalists have always argued for keeping political and economic distance between Canada and its great power patrons, Gray commented that: "A True North Strong, Free and shorn of all formal ties to a British or American imperialism, might be logical historically [he might have used the term 'ideologically' instead]—but might not be practical politics and economics."[13]

For Canada, the United States is even more important today than it was when Sutherland and Gray wrote their treatises. Two overarching realities characterize the international political system for Canada. The first is that the international system is, and for the foreseeable future will remain, unipolar. This means that the power of the United States relative to all other states in the international system is unprecedented in modern history. In a military sense, the United States has no global, or even major regional, rivals. Barry Posen has referred to America's "command of the commons"—of space, the air, and the sea. In each of these realms, the United States possesses a nearly unfettered ability to project military power without serious challenge.[14]

While American dominance is not as sweeping economically, the United States still generates between 23 and 30 percent of the total world economic product—larger than the next two countries, China and Japan, combined, and up from the 20 percent generated by the American economy in the 1980s.[15] As Allan Gotlieb, the former Canadian ambassador to the United States, has written, "transcendent U.S. power is the dominant feature of the contemporary international order." This, he notes, "renders impractical any foreign policy devoted to creating counterweights to U.S. power."[16] Professional analysis within the Canadian government concurs. The 2004 Strategic Assessment produced by the Department of National Defence's Directorate of Strategic Analysis noted that:

> In this unipolar world, the international security agenda will largely be determined by an American assessment of threats. ... There is no evidence that the European Union (EU) will develop as a counterweight to the United States, despite the aspirations of France and Germany.[17]

The second is that, even if major rivals to the United States were to emerge in the coming decades, geography ensures that Canada will still remain in the innermost ring of American power. States generally tend to characterize interests in terms of the perceived importance of particular matters to prosperity and security. For instance, in the United States, the Clinton administration envisaged American national security interests as falling to into three broad categories: "vital interests", encompassing the survival, safety and vitality of the nation; "important interests", related to national well-being and the world in which we live; and, "humanitarian interests", activated in response to humanitarian disasters or gross violations of human rights.[18]

Other administrations and other states have used such general categories as well. They provide a logical framework on which to build a consensus on Canada's national interest. Thus, Canadian interests can be divided into:

- Survival or Vital Interests: directly related to prosperity, security, and independence and *necessary* for the continuation of a free Canada and the Canadian way of life
- Major Interests: contributing to Canada's most immediate national security and prosperity objectives but not vital for the very continuation of Canada,
- Other Interests: desirable policy outcomes but usually only remotely linked to Canada's national security and prosperity[19]

Survival or Vital Interests

Survival interests are those interests associated with the continuation of the Canadian state, the society that it protects, and the Canadian way of life. Given the nature of the Canadian-American relationship and the degree to which American power shields Canada from the most serious affects of global instability, Canada's core survival interests are:

- the security of Canada and assisting in the defence of North America; and,
- maintaining and enhancing our economic relationship with the United States.

The Security of Canada and the Canadian People

The primary Canadian security interest is relatively straightforward; to ensure that Canada is able to function effectively in a manner that is commensurate with the requirement to protect the Canadian people, their way of life, and their core values. This means that the government must have capabilities at its disposal to ensure that in the event of domestic emergencies or threats to national sovereignty, it can respond quickly and effectively to counter such threats.

Given the strategic unity of North America, a related imperative is to ensure that Canada contributes effectively to the defence of North America. This is vital both to reassure the United States that Canada can defend its part of the continent without unwanted assistance, and to maximize Canadian political leverage in Washington.

Many years ago, Canadian academic Nils Orvik argued that the security and defence efforts of smaller states constituted a "defence against help" strategy. By taking care of their own security, smaller powers can ease the security concerns of larger neighbours. This contributes to the maintenance of the smaller power's sovereignty in a crisis, and minimizes the danger that a larger power would believe it necessary to violate the sovereignty of a weaker state to protect its own interests.[20]

During the Cold War, the prospect of a nuclear exchange between the United States and the Soviet Union represented the most direct threat to the survival of Canada. Canada's participation in the defence of North America and Western Europe was seen to be directly linked to the survival of Canada. Prior to the Cold War, the country's involvement in both World Wars had been perceived in similarly stark and immediate terms. With the end of the Cold War, the disappearance of the Soviet threat largely eliminated the terrible prospect of general war and potential nuclear annihilation. In that context, Colin Gray, for one, was led to conclude in 1994 that "the only plausible ... threat to Canada's survival is domestic in origin."[21]

Today, this assertion no longer seems to be valid, for it is possible to conceive of a major attack on North America involving weapons of mass destruction (WMD) that would be catastrophic for Canadian society. This might originate in the form of either a missile attack launched against the United States by a rogue state or through a terrorist attack employing a WMD device.

Many Canadians have questioned the existence of any real unconventional or terrorist threats. In 2003, even the noted Canadian military historian, Desmond Morton, rhetorically asked:

Was Canada targeted by al-Qaeda or any other terrorism? Was Montreal's Place Ville-Marie or Toronto's T-D Centre or the George Pearkes Building, the Ottawa home of the Department of National Defence, on al-Qaeda's target list? No. Had terrorists poisoned the water in Walkerton or North Battleford? No, we managed those feats ourselves. Were we afraid for our safety? Polls said no.

"The only perceptible threat to Canada in 2001," Professor Morton claimed, "came from a troubled, insecure southern neighbour, prone to the irrationality that fear produces, aggravated by media greedy for simple solutions."[22]

Yet, characteristically perhaps, this seems to put ideology ahead of a dispassionate analysis of the facts. There is fairly clear evidence that Islamic jihadists perceive Canada as a potential target. A 2002 Canadian Security and Intelligence Service report acknowledged this fact when it stated:

> Over the past decade, Canada has become increasingly involved in the campaign against Islamic extremism ... in November 2002, the media reported widely on a statement allegedly made by Osama Bin Laden in which he included Canada amongst countries deserving retribution for supporting the war on terrorism. This acknowledgment that Canada is directly threatened by terrorism is central to such a perspective.[23]

Even prior to 9/11, al-Qaeda not only identified Canada as a base for operations against the United States, but also as a potential target. The arrest of Ahmed Ressam on the Canada-U.S. border in 1999 and his subsequent revelations about plans to attack the Jewish community in Montreal, and the long-standing Hezbollah fund raising activities in Canada, are both well known.[24] Not as well known are the discoveries of *Wall Street Journal* reporter, Alan Cullison, who obtained information from the hard drives of computers used by al-Qaeda in Afghanistan, revealing that targets in Canada—namely the Israeli embassy and consulate, and Jewish cultural centres—were specifically selected to be "cased" for possible attack.[25]

The potential threat from ballistic missiles is just as real. These threats are evolving, but it is already apparent that the potential "tracks" of ballistic missiles that might be fired by potential adversaries against targets in the United States all cross over Canadian territory. Even if one questions the likelihood of such attacks in the future, the fact that the American government has already put BMD in place should have activated a strong Canadian desire to obtain a seat at the table as crucial matters related to the defence of Canada in North America are decided in Washington.

However, it did not. If a real partnership in North American defence is to be restored, the BMD issue will have to be revisited by the Canadian government at some point in the future. But, having missed the BMD boat for now, it is vital that the government at least tries to ensure that it does not make the same mistake with respect to the future maritime and land defence arrangements that are now being discussed. Otherwise, the protectorate relationship will inevitably deepen.

National Prosperity and the Canadian Way of Life

Statistics on Canada-U.S. relations illustrate the degree to which the United States acts as the anchor of Canadian prosperity and our way of life.

- Daily cross-border trade now amounts to about $2 billion per day.
- In terms of investment, 65 percent of foreign direct investment in Canada (some $228 billion in 2004) comes from the United States.[26]
- 87 percent of all Canadian exports are destined for the United States and 75 percent of all of Canada's two-way trade is conducted with the United States.[27]
- Nine of ten provinces derive a greater percentage of their GDP from trade with the United States than from trade with all the other provinces of Canada combined. (The only exception is Manitoba.)[28]
- In 2000, 63 percent of Canada's industrial output was sold to the United States while only 30 percent of that same output was sold domestically.[29]
- All told, the two-way trade with the United States in goods and services accounted for 53 percent of Canada's GDP in 2003.[30]
- Canada has a massive trade surplus with the United States, totalling nearly $140 billion in 2004.[31]

The most important characteristic of this bilateral relationship is that it is driven by ordinary Americans and Canadians who see their interests in north-south terms. Thomas Courchene has noted how the Canadian economy must increasingly be conceived as a series of north-south, rather than east-west or intra-Canadian, relationships.[32] Table 11 illustrates the stake that all of Canada's provinces have in exports alone to the U.S.

Table 11: Percentage of Provincial GDPs Generated by Exports Alone to the United States, 2001

Newfoundland and Labrador	24.3
Prince Edward Island	28.5
Nova Scotia	23.7
New Brunswick	43.3
Quebec	33.6
Ontario	48
Manitoba	24.6
Saskatchewan	26.1
Alberta	36.7
BC	22.2

From Thomas Courchene "FTA at 15, NAFTA at 10: A Canadian Perspective on North American Integration" in Thomas Courchene, Donald Savoie and Daniel Schwanen ed. *The Art of the State II: Thinking North America* (Montreal: IRPP) p. 7

During the Diefenbaker period, as well as in the Trudeau years, the government of Canada tried to resist and reverse the growth in the north-south trading relationship. The Chrétien government, in turn, did little to capitalize on the gains made by Brian Mulroney. It paid limited political attention to strengthening NAFTA's dispute settlement mechanisms, or even to trying to pre-empt the looming dispute over softwood lumber. (After all, everyone knew for years in advance that the temporary agreement on softwood was going to expire in 2001.) Instead, its primary political efforts were devoted to "Team Canada" trade missions that produced rather meagre results.

All efforts at trade diversification have failed. The depth of the bilateral Canada-U.S. trade relationship means that trying to go this route yet again is pointless. Nevertheless, it seems that pursuant to every new trade dispute with the U.S. such proposals are again trotted out. Those who do so often base such calls on the notion that Canadians "overwhelmingly reject deep integration with the United States."[33]

Yet this is simply not the case. In fact, the impetus for closer relations and the expanding network of cross-border ties is largely being driven by ordinary Canadians operating in small business concerns. It is events at the sub-national level that are determining the direction of the bilateral relationship.[34] Indeed, the anti-American sentiment and rhetoric of some Canadians notwithstanding, half of all Canadians (15 million) visit the United States for more than one day on an annual basis. About 200 million individual border crossings are recorded annually and many are business related. Cross-border telephone calls number at around 2.4 billion per year while Internet transactions are uncountable. Two-thirds of the cross-border trade actually occurs within companies that have branches on both sides of the border.[35]

Despite the heat of some rhetoric, the practical choice for most Canadians is far closer integration. The integrated nature of the North American economy means that ordinary Canadians recognize that millions of Canadian jobs, and, indeed, the entire national economy, depends on guaranteed access to the American market. The importance of deepening the bilateral relationships is widely recognized and was the featured issue at the Bush-Martin-Fox Summit in Waco, Texas in 2005. It has also been widely discussed in many Canada-U.S. forums and publications.[36]

Since 9/11, the risk that security considerations may derail this process and disrupt the present nature of the bilateral economic relationships should concern all Canadians. William Robson, of the C.D. Howe Institute, has estimated that security-related disruptions on the Canada-U.S. border might affect as much as 45 percent of Canadian exports, which support 390,000 jobs and $3.7 billion of annual investments. Others have estimated that a 10 percent increase in border costs would cut the volume of Canada-U.S. trade by 25 percent over time, and lower the net prices received by Canadian exporters by about 10 percent.[37] While the Canadian government has taken some important steps to enhance security, in some respects, politics continues to trump security in Canada; in the United States, as many have noted, it is security that trumps trade.

Therefore, the overarching objective of Canadian policy in North America must be, first to ensure that the country is inside the North American trade and security perimeter, and second to make Canada's access to the American market even more secure than it is at present. This means creating a positive environment in which a partnership relationship is valued in Washington. In such an environment, Canada will be better able to leverage and trade on its strengths, such as its oil and energy wealth, as well as the important contributions it makes to the American economy. Such realism must be the underpinning of a strong state strategy for Canada rather than a weak state strategy.

Canadian policy must make the country's vital interests in North America the foundation for Canada's broader international policy. Practical measures must then follow this recognition.

This does not mean saying "yes" to the United States on every issue, but it does mean learning to differentiate that which is a vital interest from that which is less relevant. It means that interests must trump policies that are based on ideology and emotion. It means returning to the tradition of "quiet diplomacy" that served Canada well in the 1950s and into the 1960s. It means reallocating the country's diplomatic and other resources to support what is most important. At present, as noted in Table 10, despite the overarching importance of the Canada-U.S. trading relationship, more than three times as many Canadian diplomats and officials serve in the embassies and consulates of Canada's next 20 trading partners as serve in the embassy and consulates in the United States.

To the greatest extent possible, broader international policy objectives should complement and support, and never contradict, the most important core objectives of Canadian international policy. The process of bringing greater cohesion to Canada's international policy should begin by considering what Canada's "major" and "other" interests are.

Major Interests

In contrast to vital or survival interests, while Canada's major interests certainly contribute to the country's security and prosperity, they are not usually central for the very continuation of the Canadian way of life. Changing political and strategic realities, as well as domestic political perceptions, affect which interests a state defines as vital and which it defines as major.

Our major interests are reflected in the facts governing our international trade and security choices. Canada's economic relations are evident in Table 10. All but three (Brazil, Algeria, and India) of Canada's top 21 trading partners are located in North America, Europe or the Pacific Rim, and nearly 97 percent of all Canadian trade is conducted with these three regions.

Based on these realities, one can argue that Canada's major interests related to her security and prosperity lie in three regions: Europe, the Pacific Rim, and Mexico and broader North America.

In the aftermath of 9/11 and the advent of the war on terror, which is central in United States national security policy, one can also argue that Canadian participation in this conflict is at least a major national interest and, as related to the security of North America itself, actually constitutes a vital national interest.

Europe

For both strategic and economic reasons, Europe is an area of major Canadian interest. For at least one hundred years, the maintenance of a stable balance of power in Europe has been seen as synonymous with Canada's own security interests. The domination of Europe by any hostile power has been seen as a significant threat to the security of North America. This perception lay at the heart of Canada's participation in both World Wars and the presence of Canadian troops in Europe throughout the Cold War era.

Since the end of the Cold War, the threats to European security have declined significantly and, for the first time in half a century, there are no major Canadian military deployments in Europe. While Canada retains a major interest in security developments in Russia, and the circumpolar region in particular, changing strategic circumstances and an absence of direct threats mean that Europe has declined from being an area of vital Canadian interest to a region of somewhat reduced importance.

The percentage of trade that Canada conducts with Europe has also declined over the past several decades. In 1975, Canadian trade with just the (then) nine states of the European Community constituted 10.3 percent of Canada's world trade.[38] By 2003, however, total Canadian trade with the entire European continent (some 45 states) had shrunk to only 9.6 percent of Canada's world trade. As noted in chapter three, Canada's economic profile in the major continental European states is limited—0.6 percent of Italy's world trade; 0.65 percent of Germany's, and 0.7 percent of France's.

Nevertheless, annual trade with Europe still amounts to about $46 billion USD per year, an absolute amount that is not insignificant for the Canadian economy.[39] As noted in Table 10, nine of Canada's top 21 trading partners are European countries. Foreign Direct Investment (FDI) by European countries in Canada is also significant, and includes some $58.7 billion from Great Britain and France alone—or more than 15 percent of all FDI in Canada.[40]

Canada also continues to maintain a formal treaty commitment to European security through its membership in the North Atlantic Treaty Organization (NATO). It is also a member of other European security institutions, such as the Organization for Security and Cooperation in Europe (OSCE). Such institutions, NATO in particular, are potentially useful tools for promoting some of Canada's international security interests. Likewise, since international operations often occur in a multilateral context, NATO is sometimes the institution of choice for commanding such operations, even outside of Europe.

In this regard, it is tempting for many Canadians to view NATO, and Europe, as a potential vehicle for circumventing Canada's relationship with the United States; as a means for pursuing a different agenda on the international stage from the one that is pursued in North America.[41] Rob McRae, the director general of the policy planning bureau in the Department of Foreign Affairs, wrote recently that the Canadian interest remained one of "avoid[ing] the strategic dilemma of having to chose between the US and other members of the West, whether across the Atlantic or Pacific ...." He goes on to argue that:

> The risk for Canada is that we get caught in a 'squeeze play': shut out of Europe, and ambivalent about an increasingly unilateral (or preoccupied) U.S. In this scenario, there is no 'trans-Atlantic space' which Canada can occupy, and little opportunity for us to balance our interests among traditional western partners.[42]

But in economic, political, and strategic terms, this dilemma has already arrived. Canada is of limited political and economic importance for major European states. Likewise, apart from occasional joint military missions overseas—which are usually conducted at relatively small unit levels—there is no longer any day-to-day interaction between Canadian and European militaries as there once was during the Cold War.

What has always made Canada important for Europe in a political sense has been the nature of the relationship between Ottawa and Washington. In that sense, the more political "distance" that Canada establishes from the United States, the less relevant it will be to the European states. For Canada, at every level, it is influence in Washington that matters most. Attempting to use NATO as a kind of counterweight to the United States to "establish political distance" from American policy, or to oppose it when no hard Canadian interests are at stake, is counterproductive to the national interest. It is also unlikely to meet with much success, as became evident in 2003, when Canada attempted to side with France and Germany rather than with the United States on the issue of Iraq.

Thus, there is really no option in terms of "choosing" between the U.S. and Europe. Canada is a North American, not a European power. Canadian interests begin in North America, and policies pursued in the rest of the world should be consistent with that overarching reality. In that sense, relations with neither NATO nor Europe can serve as a kind of "escape" from geographic realities. Instead, relations with Europe must be viewed as part of a larger whole; as an integral dimension in an international policy dedicated to the pursuit of the national interest, which begins in North America.

The Pacific Rim

Canada has been a Pacific power ever since British Columbia entered Confederation in 1871. However, for most of that 135-year period, the Pacific region has been somewhat neglected in Canadian international policy. Growing economic links have progressively altered that reality.[43] As indicated in Table 10, China has become Canada's second largest trading partner, with $12 billion USD in imports and $3 billion in exports in 2003. This trade deficit is matched by similar deficits with the other states of the Pacific Rim (and European countries as well). Nevertheless, 7 of Canada's top 21 trading partners are Asian/Oceania states of the Pacific Rim. Economic investment in Canada by the countries from this region—while still quite small compared to that by European nations—is growing.[44] Collectively, the Pacific Rim region has also passed Europe in terms of trade volume, with about $50 billion USD in trade in 2003; an amount that comprises around 10.1 percent of Canada's world trade.[45]

This level of economic interaction makes the region one in which Canada has a major interest. While Canada has no formal treaty obligations with respect to the security of the Pacific Rim, the continued stability of the region is a major issue of concern. The most important force for stability in the region is the United States, which directly guarantees the security of South Korea and, indirectly, the security of Taiwan. As is the case in Europe and elsewhere, the Canadian role in the Pacific Rim will inevitably be complementary to those efforts.

Mexico and Broader North America

Traditionally, Canada has not paid a great deal of attention to Mexico and the broader Americas. For instance, Canada did not join the Organization of American States (OAS) until 1990, 32 years after the organization was founded. This is partly because Canada's level of economic interaction with the Americas has always been considerably less than that with Europe or the Pacific Rim.

This is beginning to change. Canadian interest in the Americas began to increase significantly in the 1990s, with the signing of NAFTA between the United States, Canada, and Mexico in 1994. Since then, a further trade agreement has been concluded with Costa Rica, and discussions are underway related to possible agreements with the so-called Central American Four (El Salvador, Nicaragua, Honduras, and Guatemala), with the Dominican Republic, and with a number of countries in the Caribbean (CARICOM).

While some of these discussions depend on the outcome of parallel negotiations that these countries are having with the United States, the broader North American region is emerging as an area of greater interest for Canada in an economic sense. Since the signing of NAFTA, for instance, Mexico has become one of Canada's top five trading partners. In 2003, two-way trade between Canada and Mexico amounted to $9.5 billion USD, and was nearly equal to that between Canada and the United Kingdom. All told, Canadian trade with the rest of North America totals just over two percent of Canada's world trade, with

Mexico comprising most of that total.

The North American region to the south of the United States is also a relatively poor part of the world. Therefore, Canada can assist in the development of this region. Indeed, given the scope of Canada's economic activity in the Caribbean basin, there seems to be an opportunity for Canada to build on the links that already exist with this region to play a major and leading role in development efforts.

Table 12 illustrates that Canada's economic profile with some of these smaller countries is considerably greater than its profile with most of the 25 states that have been identified by the government as Canada's future principal development partners. (See Table 7 in chapter five.) Indeed, Canada usually tends to rank as a top 10 trading partner for many of these states.

Table 12: Canada's Trade, Aid, Economic, and Diplomatic Profile in Selected North American States, 2003

Country	Approximate Percentage of That State's Trade with Canada	Total Canadian Aid, 2003–2004 (millions CDN)	Approximate Numbers of Canadian Diplomatic Staff in State
Belize	0.92	$3.1	None
Dominican Republic	1.03	$2.21	4
Haiti	1.65	$23.85	14
Grenada	1.7	$2.34	None
Dominica	2.3	$3.25	None
Trinidad & Tobago	2.4	$3.89	12
Barbados	3.32	$1.39	9
Jamaica	4.7	$18.14	14
St. Kitts-Nevis	5.2	$3.67	None
Cuba	15.4	$10.79	13

Source: IMF, Direction of Trade Statistics Yearbook 2004 and CIDA, "Statistical Report on Official Development Assistance Fiscal Year 2002–03" pp. 37–44; Comparative GDP's calculated in terms of purchasing power parity found at *CIA World Fact Book* [http://www.cia.gov/cia/publications/factbook/geos/gh.html]. Canadian diplomatic staff totals include Foreign Affairs, other government employees in the embassy and consular staff. Source: Department of Foreign Affairs.

Nevertheless, none of the states mentioned in Table 12 were identified as principal Canadian development partners in 2005. Although five of the micro-states (Grenada, Trinidad and Tobago, Barbados, Dominica, and St. Kitts-Nevis) referred to above are considered "upper middle income countries", four are identified as "lower middle income" countries (Belize, Jamaica, Dominican Republic, and Cuba), and one (Haiti) is among the world's least developed countries. Despite the poverty in this region, Canadian aid levels have been modest (under $20 million per annum, and often much less), along with a relatively limited diplomatic presence.

As a North American power, Canada has the opportunity to bring much greater weight to bear in this region—similar to the role that Australia or New Zealand play in the South Pacific. This might include seeking to play a greater military role in regional stabilization missions, most notably in Haiti. In making greater efforts, Canada would not only advance its own long-term economic interests, it could make a major contribution to regional development, and assist the United States with respect to its own regional humanitarian relief, security, and stabilization efforts (perhaps relieving the United States of some of the burden in the process).

The War on Terror

While most of Canada's major interests can be defined in terms of the country's relationship to states in neighbouring regions, strategic and political imperatives can emerge from time to time that elevate certain concerns to the status of a major or even a vital interest. As the Defence Department's 2004 Strategic Assessment notes: "In this unipolar world, the international security agenda will largely be determined by an American assessment of threats."[46] The war on terror, pursued since 9/11, falls into that category.

On September 11, 2001, the world entered a new era. It did so because, with the catastrophic events of 9/11, the rules and patterns of interaction on international security matters changed. Since 9/11, security, counter-terrorism, and the prevention of another, possibly catastrophic, terrorist attack against the United States have been the principal focus of American security policy. This reality coupled with the fact that, as R.J.

Sutherland put it over 40 years ago, North America constitutes a "single target system" for any adversary[47], creates an imperative for Canadian participation.

As noted earlier, there is simply no option with respect to effective Canadian participation in the defence of Canada and North America itself. However, there may be considerable flexibility concerning the way in which Canada participates outside of North America. While the 2005 Defence Policy Statement asserts that it is desirable to meet "threats to our security as far away from our borders as possible, wherever they may arise"[48], this is actually not the *strategic imperative* that many believe, since it is almost exclusively the efforts of the United States that will do that. Indeed, the fact that the United States will automatically do that is a principal reason why Canada has not invested extensive resources in defence over the past 30 years. While a significant Canadian military and/or development effort outside of North America related to the war on terror may not be a strategic imperative, it is certainly highly *desirable politically* to be able to make such an effort.

The central focus of Canada's present efforts related to the war on terror is on Afghanistan, a country in which it had no interest prior to 9/11. Given the scope of the military and development efforts that have already been made, it is desirable to continue with those efforts. However, even at the present level of effort—over $100 million in annual aid and leading a provincial reconstruction team in Kandahar—Canada will nevertheless continue to be little more than a supporting player in Afghanistan. While this is a role similar to the one that Australia and New Zealand have played in that country, the efforts being made there by those countries are not the focal point of either state's international policy.

Efforts made in regions or countries far away from Canada will largely remain *niche contributions* to the war on terror. Yet these can be of considerable political value if used effectively. For instance, Australia's role in Iraq has been a prominent one even though its actual troop contribution has oscillated between just 800 and 2,000 troops. Both New Zealand and Norway have also made military contributions in Iraq at even more limited levels.[49]

Canada's efforts in Iraq have been largely limited to covert support behind the scenes—seconding officers to serve with the U.S. military for example. This support illustrates that the government's public opposition to the war in Iraq was never really based on legal or moral objections.

At one level, the government understood where Canadian interests lie, but domestic political factors and the ideology of the political elite were more important in setting policy. Eroding capabilities have also restricted options.

The ability of Canada to make either major or even niche contributions in times of crisis will be dependent on the resources that are allocated to advance major interests in regions of strategic importance to Canada. The identification of clear vital and major national-interest objectives, thus serves as the foundation for effective niche contributions in the rest of the world.

Other Interests

Other international policy interests are those in which preferred foreign policy outcomes may exist for Canada but which are also are less critical, in that they are only remotely linked to immediate national security and economic priorities.

Looking at the rest of the world outside of North America, Europe, and the Pacific Rim in economic terms, Canada's trading relationship with it amounts to about three percent of total world trade. Generally, and apart from the war on terror, immediate and direct security concerns in regions outside of North America, Europe, and the Pacific Rim are also usually limited.

This is not to say that Canada has absolutely no major interests in other parts of the world. Indeed, particular countries occasionally emerge to become more important than others. For instance, three states that are among Canada's top 21 trading partners are located outside of North America, Europe, and the Pacific Rim. Brazil is Canada's 14th largest trading partner, Algeria (due almost exclusively to oil) is 17th, while India ranks 21st. One-third of Canada's remaining three percent of trade with the rest of the world is conducted with just these three states.

The same is the case with respect to particular issues of concern around the world. For example, health concerns in a particular region or country may at times become an issue of direct concern to the security of Canada. Similarly, particular international trade negotiations, such as the "Free Trade of the Americas" talks, may also be of importance to the Canadian economy.

Nevertheless, in general terms, Canada's direct national interests in countries and regions outside of North America, Europe, and the Pacific Rim will usually remain limited. Adding just a few more countries to states like Brazil, Algeria and India—such as Chile and Israel, with which Canada has free trade agreements, or Saudi Arabia and Venezuela, from which Canada imports petroleum products—would soon take care of a good part of the remaining two percent of our world trade. Similarly, the Canadian capacity to become engaged in a major way in regions or countries that are far away is also quite limited, and will remain so.

In considering what Canada's other national interests might be, it is clear that the list of preferred foreign policy outcomes around the world could be endless. They might include such general goals as "security for the people of the Middle East", "dealing with weapons of mass destruction", or creating "a rule-governed international system." These may be desirable goals for any Western country, but they cannot serve as the underlying basis for Canada's international policy, because they are such long-term and general goals that they have very little concrete relevance to immediate national interests.

Yet it is exactly these types of goals that have served as the foundation for recent Canadian international policy and Canadian global engagement in most regions and international organization with almost equal (at least pretended) vigour. It is a practice that continues in the IPS. This approach to international policy has also been encouraged by many academics. Indeed, the specific objectives noted above were extolled by Jennifer Welsh in her celebrated book *At Home in the World* as exactly the types of objectives that Canada should be pursuing "with confidence" on the world stage.[50]

The problem with this approach is that it is unrealistic and irrelevant. It turns international policy on its head by making objectives that are of limited direct importance to Canada and which we only have limited influence over, the basis of international policy. This contributes to a neglect of those interests that are truly important for the security and prosperity of the country. The result is the unwitting erosion of international effectiveness, credibility, and, ultimately, national sovereignty.

When R.J. Sutherland, writing in 1962, looked ahead to the turn of the century, he forecast that Canada's traditional relationships in Europe, the Pacific Rim, and North America would continue to remain strong and probably expand. However, he counselled against the belief held by many Canadians that "they have some special affinity with the new nations of Africa and Asia." "By recognizing this fact now," he wrote, "we can at least spare ourselves from severe disillusionment."[51] Yet Canadian leaders were, of course, unaware of such counsel, and probably would have paid little attention to it had they known about it.

Ironically, the assumption that trade with the United States is strong and always will be, and that the U.S. will also protect Canada against any threats, has led governments to disregard the U.S.-Canada relationship in favour of what is peripheral. In its place, they have indulged themselves in flights of fantasy that, irony on irony, make Canada less influential, less relevant, and, ultimately, less secure.

Lastly, a word must also be said about humanitarian concerns internationally. Strictly speaking, humanitarian objectives in international policy are distinct from hard interests. They are also distinct from development objectives, which are long-term goals intended to promote stability in a way that corresponds with national interests. Nevertheless, national assets and capabilities that are principally devoted to serve military or development needs can also make a significant contribution to humanitarian relief.

Experience suggests that Canada will not consistently invest resources over the long term simply to meet global humanitarian needs. Since the national interest has been mostly excluded from Canadian aid policy, the aid budget has been cut whenever domestic circumstances have so demanded. This occurred in both the Mulroney and Chrétien governments.

The best way to ensure that the nation has the capacity to address humanitarian needs is to acquire the hard capabilities (military, intelligence, and development assets) that are needed to advance national interest objectives. In that way, the humanitarian needs that inevitably arise within countries and regions important to Canada, and elsewhere, can be tackled more effectively.

Summary

This chapter proposes a new way of looking at Canadian international policy. Such an approach is essential to making Canada an effective actor on the international stage rather than simply an object that is affected by international events and has little influence over them. Canada must endeavour to become a strong state rather than a weak one that is increasingly little more than a protectorate of its larger neighbour. Based on the different ways in which countries such as New Zealand, Norway, and Australia have approached their international policy, there are several options available to Canada to pursue such a "strong-state strategy."

— NOTES —

[1] John Ibbitson *The Polite Revolution: Perfecting the Canadian Dream* (Toronto: McClelland and Stewart, 2005) p. 1

[2] Lloyd Axworthy, "Time to Refine Ties with U.S." *Toronto Star* (August 22, 2005); Allan Woods "Revisit NAFTA: Harper" *National Post* (September 8, 2005); CTV.ca [news online] "Canada Must Strengthen Ties with China: McCallum" (October 16, 2005).

[3] See for instance, Paul Vieira "Canada Barely Blip on Radar of China's Business Sector" *National Post* (September 15, 2005) p. FP5

[4] Canada. *Canada's International Policy Statement—A Role of Pride and Influence in the World, Overview* (2005) pp. 4–5

[5] Definition found at: [http://en.wikipedia.org/wiki/National_interest]

[6] Canada. *Canada's International Policy Statement—A Role of Pride and Influence in the World, Overview* (2005) p. 5

[7] John Ibbitson, *The Polite Revolution* p. 202

[8] Michael Ignatieff, "Peace Order and Good Government: A Foreign Policy Agenda for Canada" Skelton Lecture, Department of Foreign Affairs and International Trade, 12 March 2004

[9] W.D. Macnamara and Ann Fitz-Gerald "A National Security Framework for Canada" in Hugh Segal ed. *Geopolitical Integrity* (Montreal: IRPP, 2005) p. 97

[10] For instance, see discussion by Rob Huebert "Failed and Failing States: The Core Threat to Canadian Security? *In the Canadian Interest? Assessing Canada's International Policy Statement*" (Canadian Defence and Foreign Affairs Institute, November 2005) pp. 69–73

[11] R.J. Sutherland "Canada's Long Term Strategic Situation" *International Journal* XVII (Summer 1962): 201

[12] Ibid: 204

[13] Colin S. Gray, *Canadian Defence Priorities: A Question of Relevance* (Toronto: Clarke, Irwin and Company, 1972) p. 14

[14] Barry Posen, "Command of the Commons: The Military Foundations of US Hegemony" *International Security* 28 (Summer 2003): pp. 5–46. The massive technological lead of the United States is a key part of US hegemony; it is a condition which is likely to be sustained for some time since, as Posen pointedly notes, American military Research and Development spending *alone* equals the *total* defence spending of France and Germany combined while it exceeds *total* Chinese defence spending.

[15] The CIA measured the U.S. share of the world product as 29.5 percent in 2001. Others have suggested that the true figure is somewhat lower. Barry Posen for instance has estimated a figure of 23 percent. See Barry Posen, "Command of the Commons: The Military Foundation of US Hegemony": 10; The Chicago Council on Foreign Relations also uses the figure of 30 percent. As a further indication of American dominance, U.S. stock markets are the most important in the world, accounting for 36 percent of the global market value. The United States also remains the centre for global research and technological development–75 percent of all Nobel laureates in the sciences, economics and medicine do research and live in the United States. Chicago Council on Foreign Relations, *Global Views 2004. (ccfr.org/globalviews2004/sub/usa.htm)*

[16] Allan Gotlieb, "Romanticism and Realism in Canada's Foreign Policy" (Toronto: C.D. Howe Institute, Benefactors Lecture, November 3, 2004) p. 31

[17] Department of National Defence. Directorate of Strategic Analysis. Policy Planning Division. Policy Group *Strategic Assessment, 2004* p. 13

[18] Cited by W.D. Macnamara and Ann Fitz-Gerald "A National Security Framework for Canada" p. 89

[19] Adapted from Colin S. Gray, *Canadians in a Dangerous World* (Toronto: Atlantic Council of Canada, 1994) p. 19; and, W.D. Macnamara and Ann Fitz-Gerald "A National Security Framework for Canada" p. 100

[20] Nils Orvik "Defence Against Help –A Strategy for Small States?" *Survival* Vol. 15 No. 5 (September-October, 1973) pp. 228-31

[21] Colin S. Gray, *Canadians in a Dangerous World* p. 19

[22] Desmond Morton, *Understanding Canadian Defence* (Montreal: A Penguin McGill Book, 2003) pp. 23–24

[23] Canadian Security Intelligence Service, *2002 Public Report,* Part I - Global Security Environment

[24] Ressam was arrested with a trunk full of explosives as he tried to enter the United States with the intent of launching a major attack on the Los Angeles

airport. See: Stewart Bell, *Cold Terror: How Canada Nurtures and Exports Terrorism Around the World* (John Wiley and Sons, 2004) pp. 132–140 and 79–102.

[25] Alan Cullison, "Inside Al-Qaeda's Hard Drive", *The Atlantic*, 294 (September 2004): 68;

[26] *Canada's International Policy Statement: A Role of Pride and Influence in the World* Overview Paper (2005) p. 2 and Commerce Paper p. 10.

[27] Speaking Notes for the Hon. Perrin Beatty, President and CEO of the Canadian Manufacturers and Exporters, "Isolation or Integration: Canada's Role in North America" (August 28, 2002) p. 3

[28] Thomas Courchene "FTA at 15, NAFTA at 10: A Canadian Perspective on North American Integration" in Thomas Courchene, Donald Savoie and Daniel Schwanen ed. *The Art of the State II: Thinking North America* (Montreal: IRPP, 2005) pp. 7

[29] Speaking Notes for the Hon. Perrin Beatty, President and CEO of the Canadian Manufacturers and Exporters, "Isolation or Integration: Canada's Role in North America" (August 28, 2002) p. 3

[30] William Robson, *The North American Imperative: A Public Good Framework for Canada-U.S. Economic and Security Cooperation*, (C.D. Howe Commentary, Border Papers Series, October 2004) pp.13–14

[31] *Canada's International Policy Statement: A Role of Pride and Influence in the World* Commerce Paper (2005) p. 10

[32] See: Thomas Courchene "FTA at 15, NAFTA at 10: A Canadian Perspective on North American Integration"

[33] Council of Canadians "What Canadians Told Us" (June 2005).

[34] See for a discussion of growing provincial and state links see Dieudonne Mouafo "Regional Dynamics in Canada-United States Relations" (Paper prepared for the 2004 Conference of the Canadian Political Science Association University of Manitoba, Winnipeg, June 3, 2004); For a discussion of cross-border environmental ties see: Debora L. Van Nijnatten "The Constituent Regions of the Canada-United States Environmental Relationship" in George A. MacLean ed. *Canada and the United States: A Relationship at a Crossroads?* (Bision Paper 7, University of Manitoba, December 2005) pp. 103-116.

[35] Michael Hart, "A New Accommodation with the United States: The Trade and Economic Dimension" *The Art of the State: Thinking North America* (IRPP Vol. 2 No. 2, 2005) pp. 25–26 and William Robson, *The North American*

Imperative: A Public Good Framework for Canada-U.S. Economic and Security Cooperation p. 6

[36] Discussions of options for deepening the bilateral economic relationship can be found in: William Robson, *The North American Imperative: A Public Good Framework for Canada-U.S. Economic and Security Cooperation*, pp. 15-28: Council on Foreign Relations—Independent Task Force on the Future of North America "Creating a North American Community" (2005); Wendy Dobson, Shaping the Future of the North American Economic Space: A Framework for Action (C.D. Howe Commentary, Border Papers Series, April 2002); Woodrow Wilson International Center for Scholars, Canada Institute, Mexico Institute, Project on America and the Global Economy "Toward a North American Community? A Conference Report" (Washington, D.C.: 2002).

[37] William Robson, *The North American Imperative: A Public Good Framework for Canada-U.S. Economic and Security Cooperation*, p.13

[38] Roy Rempel, *Counterweights: The Failure of Canada's German and European Policy, 1955–1995* (Montreal: McGill-Queen's University Press, 1996) p. 101.

[39] International Monetary Fund, *Direction of Trade Statistics Yearbook 2004* pp. 119–20

[40] *Canada's International Policy Statement: A Role of Pride and Influence in the World* Commerce Paper (2005) p. 10. The relative importance of Canada in the foreign investment activity of these states needs to be put in perspective however. For instance, already in 1995, British overseas investment totalled nearly 700 billion pounds (c. $1.4 trillion CDN) .Since British overseas investment has grown in the past decade, the $30 billion of British investment in Canada in 2004 certainly constitutes less than two percent of this total. Source: United Kingdom. HM Treasury: [http://archive.treasury.gov.uk/pub/html/top/top8/sum.html]

[41] See for instance: Captain (N) Peter Avis "Seductive Hegemon: Why NATO Is Still Important to Canada" *Canadian Military Journal* (Spring 2004): pp. 15–22

[42] Rob McRae "International Policy Reviews in Perspective" *Canada Among Nations 2004* p. 64

[43] This has been supported by increasing Asian immigration. Over one million Canadians are now of Chinese descent—a number that continues to grow.

[44] Total FDI by China and Japan in Canada was about $10 billion in 2004. *Canada's International Policy Statement: A Role of Pride and Influence in the*

World Commerce Paper (2005) p. 16

[45] Total comprises Canada's two-way trade with 21 states, excluding Mexico and the United States, of the Asia-Pacific Economic Cooperation (APEC) forum. International Monetary Fund, *Direction of Trade Statistics Yearbook 2004* p. 120

[46] Department of National Defence. Directorate of Strategic Analysis. Policy Planning Division. Policy Group *Strategic Assessment, 2004* p. 13

[47] R.J. Sutherland "Canada's Long Term Strategic Situation": 204

[48] *Canada's International Policy Statement: A Role of Pride and Influence in the World* Defence Paper (2005) p. 2

[49] As was the case with both New Zealand and Norwegian policy, Canada could certainly have been more visible and supportive after the invasion. If the condition of the Canadian military ruled out an operational role, then the provision of engineers for reconstruction (as provided by New Zealand) or a field hospital would have allowed Canada to play a tangible supporting role.

[50] Jennifer Welsh, *At Home in the World: Canada's Global Vision for the 21st Century* (Toronto: Harper Collins, 2004) pp. 19-20

[51] R.J. Sutherland "Canada's Long Term Strategic Situation": 206

CONCLUSION

Climbing Back From Protectorate to Partner

I ask *Canada to take another look at your centuries-old friend, the*
one you'll have to live next door to for time eternal, the one you know
would be the first on the scene in your time of need.

–David Wilkins, U.S. ambassador to Canada

Canada is evolving into a *de facto* protectorate of the United States. We
are approaching this humiliating international status because the country's leaders have had a poor sense of the national interest and an ideologically skewed approach to international relations. In essence, Canadian decision-makers have been living in a dreamland largely of their own making.

The move toward full protectorate status is occurring in stages, resulting in a gradual deterioration of Canada's sovereignty. The first stage in
that process, limited Canadian political leverage in Washington, even on
important bilateral issues, is already apparent. Washington perceives
Canada as both irrelevant and unreliable, and this perception is, increasingly, leading Washington to make unilateral decisions on issues of vital
and major interest. This loss of respect for Canadian interests may eventually lead Washington simply to dictate to Ottawa policy that, owing
to the asymmetrical nature of the relationship, Canada will be obliged
to implement.

How far Canada has progressed down the road toward being a protectorate is a matter for debate. Fortunately, however, Canada is not doomed
to such an end. While Canada is a small power relative to the United
States, size does not automatically connote dependency or protectorate
status. Instead, a partnership relationship is feasible. But it can only rest
on a foundation of sound and realistic policy-making.

To avoid protectorate status, Canada must move away from a "weak
state" approach to international policy making. This requires a policy
environment in which political and bureaucratic decision-making is

capable of identifying and advancing the national interest in a coherent fashion. It requires public discussion and debate so that a national consensus can begin to emerge on the types of policies, objectives, and capabilities needed to advance national interest objectives effectively. Such a "strong-state" approach to policy making must involve the reform of Canada's decision-making institutions to do the following:

- Facilitate the development of a serious national strategic culture that, to the greatest extent possible, removes ideology from international policy and ensures that international policy reflects the interests of all Canadians rather than the views of a select few.

- Make international policy as non-partisan as possible, based on the recognition that the partisan interests of the country's political parties cannot act as a substitute for the national interest.

- Build a long-term policy consensus that recognizes that a close partnership with the United States must be first priority of Canadian international policy; that such a partnership must serve as the foundation of effective and lasting sovereignty and as a central vehicle for Canada's wider international role.

Reformed national decision-making structures must rest on the foundation of professional and non-partisan policy-making. Within the executive branch this must begin with the establishment of bodies capable of "speaking truth to power" to the government. These new institutions must be complemented by fundamental reforms designed to make Parliament more effective, able to provide real oversight, and truly representative of all Canadians.

Canadian interests can probably be served by three alternative approaches with respect to capabilities and resources. As discussed in chapter six, these encompass a minimalist, a mid-level, or a maximum option. Each of these approaches would seek to focus diplomatic, military, and development efforts on the objectives that are defined as most important to the national interest. Policies and objectives irrelevant to the national interest, and particularly those running counter to it, would be discarded.

Minimalist option: This approach would focus Canada's efforts and resources on supporting the country's key survival and vital interests vis-à-vis the United States. Pursuing such a minimalist option would entail limited costs, and principally involve the creation of more professional and more effective national decision-making structures, a more rational use of existing resources, and the complementary reform of national political institutions.

With proper political leadership, minimalist objectives could probably be achieved in relatively short order—a few years. But with a refocus on resources on North America, the ability of Canada to influence or respond to events outside the continent, other than in the most symbolic fashion, would naturally be limited.

Mid-level option: Such an approach would build on the measures undertaken to achieve the minimalist option, but with an added and better ability to advance major interests outside of North America.

The increased resources and capabilities required to pursue such a mid-level strategy should not be underestimated since they would require, for the Canadian Forces for example, a much greater emphasis on power projection capability than currently exists. Given the present state of Canada's national capabilities (not just military, but also the current dispersed nature of Canadian development efforts, the complete absence of any intelligence capability, and the dispersal of diplomatic efforts) such an approach will likely take 7 to 10 years of concerted effort to implement effectively.

Maximum option: This approach would require the most concerted effort and the greatest resources. It would encompass taking on a leadership role in selected areas, for example with respect to development efforts in countries in which Canada can identify major interests and the ability to make a significant difference.

While the resources required to implement such an approach would be significant, efforts would nevertheless still have to be concentrated on those areas in which the national interest is significant. This option would take the longest time to implement since it involves not only the acquisition of major capabilities, but also the buildup of considerable political credibility in those capitals in which it matters most. When one considers that some Australian military capabilities, first identified as required in the Defence White Paper of 2000, will not achieve operational status until about 2015, a time-frame of 15 to 20 years for a similar Canadian transformation (that is out to about 2025) is not unrealistic.

It is readily apparent that if Canada decides to move toward a maximum option, it must begin with a minimalist approach. In that respect, the implementation of minimalist approach would seem to be the first step toward restoring Canada's international effectiveness, whether one sees the move toward the medium or maximum options as required by the national interest or not.

The first step toward implementing any of these approaches is a recognition that Canada's past approach to international affairs has not only been unrealistic, it has served the country badly and is leading inexorably toward a loss of national sovereignty. While breaking with the failed policies of the recent past will be difficult, requiring both major reforms and a change in thinking, the consequences of not doing so are dire.

Understanding the factors that lie at the heart of Canada's present national condition is the central to constructing a more serious and effective national strategic culture and to restoring credibility in Canada's international policy. It is also the essential prerequisite for elevating Canada back to the status of a real partner, rather than a protectorate, within North America.

INDEX

The "n" in page numbers indicates endnote number.

AUTHOR

Roy Rempel was a foreign and defence policy advisor on Parliament Hill for nearly four years and holds a Ph.D. in international relations from Queen's University and a Masters degree from the University of Manitoba. He held a Volkswagen Fellowship at the German Historical Institute/American Center for Contemporary German Studies in Washington D.C. as well as a North Atlantic Treaty Organization (NATO) Fellowship.

Rempel taught international relations at Memorial University in St. John's, Newfoundland, from 1994 to 1998. He has published numerous academic papers on Canadian defence, foreign and strategic policies and is the author of two prior books, *Counterweights* (McGill-Queen's 1996) and *The Chatter Box* (Breakout-Dundurn 2002).